30 DAYS
TO A HAPPY EMPLOYEE

How a Simple Program of Acknowledgment
Can Build Trust and Loyalty at Work

DOTTIE BRUCE GANDY

With a Foreword by Jack Lowe, Jr.

A Fireside Book
Published by Simon & Schuster
New York   London   Toronto   Sydney   Singapore

FIRESIDE
Rockefeller Center
1230 Avenue of the Americas
New York, NY 10020

Designed by William Ruoto

Manufactured in the United States of America

1 3 5 7 9 10 8 6 4 2

Library of Congress Cataloging-in-Publication Data
Gandy, Dottie Bruce.
30 days to a happy employee : how a simple program of acknowledgment can
build trust and loyalty at work / Dottie Bruce Gandy.
p. cm.
"A Fireside book."
1. Job satisfaction. 2. Personnel management. I. Title.

HF5549.5.J63 G627 2001
658.3'14—dc21

2001020069

ISBN 0-684-87329-X

In loving memory of my father, Basel Bruce
March 5, 1913–June 14, 2000

AUTHOR'S NOTE

My fascination with the subject of acknowledgment showed up at an early age in my life. It seemed to be influenced by the fact that I was half of a set of identical twins. We were so identical, in fact, that we used to joke that even our parents couldn't tell us apart until we were twelve. While being an identical twin resulted in lots of attention directed our way, that attention was always *jointly* focused.

Consciously or unconsciously, at some point in our lives, we found ourselves wanting to be acknowledged for our differences, rather than our identical looks. We started to exhibit the kind of competitive behavior that would call attention to us as individuals. We sought out those activities that would distinguish us one from the other. So determined were we to create our own identities that our life paths took almost opposite tracks.

Sadly, the need for such a focused effort ended with Nancy's untimely death from cancer in 1993. That which had propelled me to distinguish myself from another no longer existed.

The desire to be acknowledged, however, remained.

It goes without saying that this book is dedicated to Nancy Bruce Fite, without whose identical presence in my life for fifty-three years this book might not have been written.

FOREWORD

This is a book about acknowledgment. Not the kind of acknowledgment associated with reward and recognition programs (which seek to compensate employees for what they do), but, rather, the kind of acknowledgment that honors who we are. Each of us has qualities of character that transcend the jobs we hold or the skills we have mastered. Business experts have told us for a long time that it is *these* traits for which we long to be affirmed. Somehow, when these qualities are validated, especially in the workplace, performance, productivity, loyalty, and happiness also transcend their preexisting levels.

There is no shortage of surveys that tell us what employees want most is to know that what they contribute matters to their company. In many instances their happiness on the job is contingent on getting this kind of feedback. Regretfully, the feedback, if it comes at all, is usually in the form of a written performance review once a year, or the very occasional pat on the back. Those of us who consider ourselves to be compassionate and caring employers know that this simply isn't enough.

Many well-meaning organizations stay stuck in the knowledge that more needs to be done without ever taking the kind of action that produces the desired results. In other words, it is easy to reach consensus that more needs to be done, but we falter when translating this knowledge into action.

In her book, Dottie has made this transition easy for us. You will be introduced to what she calls the *30-Day Process,* a deceptively simple method for moving us from the occasional act of kindness to an intentional and sustaining way of interacting with those around us that leaves them—and us—feeling connected to our true worth.

The litmus test for such communication comes when we have the courage to ask those whom we employ how we're doing when it comes to making everyone feel valued. One such test for our company, TDIndustries, started three years ago when we first applied for consideration for *Fortune* magazine's "100 Best Companies to Work For." The qualification process for this designation is rigorous, with two-thirds of the scoring based on what our Partners (that's what we call employees at TDIndustries) say on their surveys. You can imagine how honored we felt when their responses landed us in the top ten on *Fortune*'s list for four consecutive years.

Some might be quick to say that it's leadership that dictates such results. At TDIndustries, however, we know that it is leadership's *willingness to serve those whom they employ* that makes the difference. If our Partners feel valued for who they are as well as what they contribute, it's because they know those of us in leadership have as our first priority *their* needs. To get the performance we need from our Partners, we expect servant leadership *and* business results from our managers.

About six months ago I was visiting with one of our construction mechanics about these dual expectations. He had been with us about seven years and had worked for several different supervisors during that time. He told me that most of his supervisors had really been great. They had treated him with respect and had regularly given him reinforcement and acknowledgment of his accomplishments. He said that when he worked for these supervisors, he had given them "all I've got."

He went on to say that two of his supervisors had treated him quite differently. The only feedback he got from them was disrespectful and negative. When he worked for those two supervisors, he had given them "the least I have to in order to keep my job."

The main reason to expect supervisors to treat people with respect and to offer regular acknowledgment and encouragement is because it is the right way to treat another human being. But more important, we cannot afford supervisors who are getting "the least I have to in order to keep my job." The difference between that and "all I've got" is a tremendous competitive disadvantage. Knowing that our Partners feel valued and acknowledged for what they contribute *is* our competitive advantage.

For about thirty years we have had a very comprehensive Leadership Development effort centered around Robert Greenleaf's *The Servant as Leader.* Simply stated, Greenleaf says that the legitimate route to leadership is a desire to serve those led and that the test of leadership is the growth of those served.

Most new learnings are obvious in hindsight. We learned the need for leadership preparation and about servant leadership from Robert Greenleaf. I believe that a high-trust culture is critical for any organization making the changes and possessing the agility required in today's rapidly changing world. Dottie Gandy is now teaching us the power of acknowledgment in building a high-trust culture in *30 Days to a Happy Employee.*

What Dottie offers the reader is a viable way to serve those whom we employ by honoring who they are as human beings. For those of you who feel such an approach is soft, I urge you to read on before drawing any conclusions. Her approach is as unique as it is useful. The book is filled with stories and anecdotes about individuals and organizations that have both risen—and failed to rise—to the "acknowledgment" occasion, with predictable results. In other words, she has done her homework.

I have known Dottie Gandy for quite a few years through the work of Stephen Covey, a good friend and Dottie's former employer. We have used her extensively as a speaker and presenter at TDIndustries. As an employee-owned company, we are selective about the people we choose to work with our Partners. For example, Stephen Covey and Tom Peters have both presented to our company. Covey's teachings, coupled with Dottie's talents, have had a very significant impact on our efforts to significantly improve the leadership capabilities of us all. *30 Days to a Happy Employee* is another wonderful gift from Dottie to those of us striving to build organizations that allow the human beings working in them to be as great as they all want to be.

With this new gift from Dottie, I am confident the leaders at TDIndustries will be better able to fulfill our leadership expectations and that we will even more often get "all I've got" from our Partners.

This book is more than an idea whose time has come; the message is, in fact, long overdue. I urge you to read this book and find out for yourselves what happens when you take the time to truly honor those whom you employ.

—JACK LOWE, JR.
CEO, TDINDUSTRIES, DALLAS, TEXAS

ACKNOWLEDGMENTS

As many of you know, it is impossible for any of us to be who and what we are without the support and nurturing of a large number of people in our lives. This is truly borne out when one writes a book, especially her first. *30 Days to a Happy Employee* is a team effort in the truest sense of that phrase. And for that reason I take joy and pleasure in acknowledging those who have been my "partners" in the process called life and the writing of this book.

The acknowledgments that follow are in no particular order, and, to paraphrase most Academy Award winners in their acceptance speeches, "I know I'm probably going to leave someone out . . ." Nonetheless, the groups and individuals I am listing are responsible, as much as myself, for the quality and message of this book. Please take a few moments to join me in celebrating their contributions.

I express my gratitude to:

My mom, Cathryn Bruce, and my late father, Basel Bruce, who are and were models for what it is to offer unconditional love.

Kelly, Kyle, Alex, and Collin Newman, otherwise known as my daughter, son-in-law, and two extraordinary grandchildren, who remind me daily of the importance of having a family in which everyone feels appreciated and valued, regardless of age.

Rebecca Lopinto, my younger daughter, for being an exceptional teacher and an extraordinary human being, and for her children, Mike and Christina Lopinto, the first to call me "Grandottie."

Tom, whose loving presence as a marriage partner sees only possibility in me.

Kathy, Jay, Ben, Sam, Kristin, Rich, Traci, Trevor, Don, Mavolen, Junie, and Clyde, for keeping me in touch with how blessed I am to have a large, close-knit family; and my late Uncle Sam.

Brad Gandy, the only (step)son I've ever known, who offered acceptance at the very time I needed it.

Dr. Stephen R. Covey, who is one of about four people I know who truly walk their talk.

Denise Cavanaugh, Howard Ross, and Sharon Fox Hasley, who taught me the joys of having really great business partners.

Don Cook, for cocreating Kelly and Rebecca with me.

The group of people who attended the Edwene Gaines Prosperity Seminar with me in Mentone, Alabama, where I first said out loud, "I'm going to write a book."

My fellow apostles, friends, board members, and staff at the Unity Church of Dallas, who have cheered, supported, and nurtured me from the beginning about this book—especially our senior minister, David McClure, who has been declaring this book a best-seller from the pulpit for two years!

Every person who attempted and/or completed the 30-Day Process, or some variation of it, as a part of this book's research, and who lovingly and patiently provided me with feedback.

Bruce Lowe, Jack Lowe, Jr., Doug Hawthorne, Gary Johnson, Wayne Scott, Marie Kellam, Lloyd Linville, and Dennis Newgren, for finding many ways to help me succeed in business—and in life.

The organizations that generously agreed to test the workshops that helped validate the premise of this book.

David Hale Smith, my literary agent, who convinced me we had a chance with this book and went out and found Simon & Schuster as proof.

Caroline Sutton, the editor at Simon & Schuster who made it so easy for me to be a novice author and who models what it is to be a friend and coach as well as an editor.

Roice Krueger, Sam Thurston, Pam Walsh, Eric Harvey, Jerry Magar, John Knight, Joyce Shuman, Sally Craig, Linda DuVall, Leslie Guttenberg, Sheri Walters, Beverly Upton, Dale Stevens, Alexandra Armstrong, friends along the way who made—and make—a difference in my life.

My friends at Pathways, especially Class 157, who became spiritual coauthors of this book.

The late Israel Cohen—and all of my friends at Giant Food—for teaching me what it means to be loved and accepted, no matter what.

Jan Belcher, whose willingness to meet me at the gym every weekday at 6:00 A.M. keeps me on track—literally!

Finally, I want to thank all of you who as a result of reading this book will take the initiative to transform your workplace, your family, and the lives of those around you by mastering the habit of acknowledgment.

CONTENTS

INTRODUCTION

NEXT TO PHYSICAL SURVIVAL, THE GREATEST NEED OF A HUMAN
BEING IS . . . TO BE AFFIRMED, TO BE VALIDATED, TO BE
APPRECIATED.
    —DR. STEPHEN R. COVEY, *THE SEVEN HABITS OF*
        HIGHLY EFFECTIVE PEOPLE

Few of us would argue that in our most quiet and reflective
moments, we suspect—or perhaps know—that underneath
it all we are innately good people. I believe it is in these
moments that we wonder if others see this in us as well. And
thus we warm to hearing our goodness validated or affirmed
by those around us, especially those who mean the most
to us.

The warmth cools, however, when we bump up against
at least two learned beliefs: The first is that it is rude to come
right out and ask others what qualities they admire in us; the
second is that our self-worth is less dependent on what others think about us than on what we think about ourselves.
While I concur that there is some validity to the *intentions*
behind these beliefs, I also believe that to embrace them

exclusively, independent of the input of others, limits our getting what we want and deserve from others, an ongoing validation that our goodness is seen and valued by those who are most important to us.

As human beings we are greatly underacknowledged and underappreciated. The irony is that we didn't start out that way. As infants, we received an almost unlimited amount of positive feedback and attention. Even our burps and wails were oohed and aahed over by adults whose behavior made us believe that our every movement and utterance was something special. Someone has said that we see children as geniuses because they haven't been hypnotized by limitations. Somewhere along the way, however, the very things for which we used to be praised began to be ignored—or worse yet, we were chastised for them. We slowly but surely learned that who we are in and of ourselves is not praiseworthy; that we must now exhibit approved-of learned behaviors if we are to continue to receive a positive response.

Eventually, absent some kind of sustained affirming input, we tend to disconnect from our intrinsic qualities. We choose instead to believe the social mirrors that constantly compare us to impossible norms. As a result, that which we know to be good about ourselves becomes mired in self-imposed criticism from which we rarely allow ourselves to recover. Thus, the reminder from another of the qualities we possess becomes a powerful connector that intrudes most effectively on those self-imposed limitations.

It is not my intention in this book to provide a mass of psychological data that confirm our need to be validated. I am not qualified to do so, nor do I believe such information is necessary to support the premise of this book—namely, that it is in our own and others' best interest to provide some kind of ongoing, sustaining affirmation of the value and contributions of those around us.

Much of this book is focused on the workplace, since surveys have shown for a long time that we are missing the mark at the organizational level when it comes to affirming the contributions of employees. Employees are the folks who make it possible for a business to make a profit, keep its customers, and go about the day-to-day routine of keeping the doors open and the company running.

Another reason this book targets employers as the logical starting place is that corporate America is one of the most influential places I know of for getting the word out to as many people as possible that they are valued, appreciated, and acknowledged. This is because sooner or later most of us wind up in the workplace. The amount of time we spend in our home environments, growing up or in school, is usually much shorter than the amount of time we spend working.

Selfishly stated, I want to reach as many readers as possible, and I believe that focusing on the work environment can accomplish that. That admission notwithstanding, I am also committed to showing what happens when acknowledgment begins at home, as Chapter 11 will demonstrate.

I don't know about you, but I like the idea that others see in me the qualities I like about myself—and are willing to tell me so. This doesn't mean that I am not a whole person without other people's input. Rather, it means simply that I enjoy knowing that some of the qualities I have consciously chosen to develop are noticed and appreciated by others.

And I want others to know that I admire and appreciate the virtues that make them special to me.

I am hopeful that the 30-Day Process of acknowledgment introduced in this book will be a useful mechanism for nudging us in the direction of getting the job done when it comes to celebrating the good news about us.

30 DAYS
TO A HAPPY EMPLOYEE

CHAPTER ONE

BEYOND THE PAYCHECK . . . FOR A REASON

Everyone has an invisible sign hanging from their neck saying "Make me feel important."
—Mary Kay Ash

Charles Plumb, a U.S. Naval Academy graduate, was a jet pilot during the Vietnam War. After seventy-five combat missions, his plane was destroyed by a surface-to-air missile. Plumb safely ejected and parachuted into enemy territory. He was captured and spent six years in a Communist Vietnamese prison. He survived the ordeal and now lectures on the lessons he learned from that experience.

One day, when Plumb and his wife were sitting in a restaurant, a man at another table came up and said, "You're Plumb! You flew jet fighters in Vietnam from the aircraft carrier *Kitty Hawk*. You were shot down!"

Somewhat surprised, Plumb asked, "How in the world did you know that?"

The man replied, "I packed your parachute."

Plumb gasped in surprise and gratitude. The man pumped his hand and said, "I guess it worked."

"It sure did. If the chute you packed hadn't worked, I wouldn't be here today," Plumb responded.

Plumb couldn't sleep that night, thinking about that man. He says, "I kept wondering what he might have looked like in a navy uniform: a white hat, a bib in the back, and bell-bottom trousers. I wonder how many times I might have seen him and not even said good morning, how are you, or anything else, because, you see, I was a fighter pilot, and he was just a sailor."

Now Plumb asks his audiences, "Who's packing your parachute?"

Plumb's story is a compelling reminder that our lives are richer and our work easier because of those who are committed to doing what is asked of them and doing it well. Surely they are worthy of our recognition.

Experts of all kinds have told us for years that next to physical survival, one of our deepest needs as human beings is to be affirmed or validated for who we are and what we contribute.

Nowhere is this more dramatically demonstrated than in the workplace. For at least the last twenty-five years, business surveys have reminded us that one of the main reasons employees *voluntarily* leave their jobs is that they do not feel valued for their contributions in human terms. Robert Half International Inc., for example, reports that as many as 25 percent of good employees who quit their jobs cite a lack of appreciation as their reason. With the average national job turnover at 2.7 million a year, thanks in part to the lure of start-up companies, the problem is approaching a near-crisis level.

In 1999, when *Inc.* magazine announced its annual list of the five hundred fastest-growing companies in the nation, 47 percent of those named said that not being able to attract and keep qualified employees was their *number one* inhibitor to growth.

The conclusion to be drawn is fairly simple: Employees who feel acknowledged for who they are and what they contribute tend to stay with their organizations. Those who don't, leave.

While some of those who leave say they are doing so for more money or a more impressive title, it takes little probing to realize that what many of them are really telling us is "Maybe if I earn more money or have a fancier title, I will *feel* more valued." They arrive at their new jobs full of hope. However, absent a culture that provides some authentic validation of who they are and what they contribute, their frustration surfaces all over again, and for many the job search resumes.

The irony of this chase for recognition is that employees have come to accept the fact that they will probably spend their working years being underacknowledged and underappreciated. They learn to settle for a work environment that asks much and gives back much less. That such an approach is costly to employers seems to be incidental to avoiding the challenge of taking the (inexpensive) time to let the people they count on the most know just that.

From my perspective, it seems almost insane to think that businesses would spend more and more of their budget dollars on expensive reward and recognition programs that get a much lower return on employee productivity than they would to institute a culture where individuals are routinely honored and productivity soars. This alone argues for a new approach.

What seems to be missing is the kind of acknowledgment that inspires employees to perform at extraordinary levels; that engenders the kind of loyalty that ensures rather than impedes growth; that results in a corporate culture founded on respect for the individual.

Even the enlightened workplaces that recognize the need to provide such a culture seem to flounder when it comes to implementation. At best they look for more and more ways to honor employees through elaborate reward and recognition programs, heaping expensive gifts and extravagant travel on the few who are fortunate enough to be singled out for honor. What they fail to do, however, is let their employees know, across the board and on a day-to-day basis, that who they are matters and what they contribute makes a difference.

I'm talking about the simplicity of saying something like "I know we ask a lot of you, and I can't see that changing. What I want you to know, however, is how much we appreciate who you are and your willingness to show up every day and do your job well." Over and over again while I was collecting data for this book, employees said they would happily trade the occasional gift/trip for a job done well for a sincere, repeated pat on the back that would let them know their efforts are appreciated.

One employee who voluntarily left his position with a well-known nonprofit organization because he didn't feel his efforts were acknowledged said, "I would have stayed for a smile."

This book offers a unique 30-Day Process that responds to our desire to provide the kind of acknowledgment that gives us what we seek from those who matter most—a reminder that we are intrinsically good people worthy of such appreciation. Specifically, the 30-Day Process extends an invitation to see the contributions and qualities of others in a way that we have never done, one that goes beyond the obvious to the intrinsic.

This is not a book about reward and recognition. This is a book about acknowledgment. The distinction lies in the outcome. If what you are seeking is short-term, temporary loyalty, reward and recognition programs will suffice. If you are looking for long-term sustainable improvement in workplace performance and retention, acknowledgment is the key.

The 30-Day Process explained later in this book invites us to share, face-to-face, a different quality or trait that we admire and appreciate about another person—every day for thirty days. (For those of you who blanch at the thought of promising to do *anything* for thirty days, hang on until you know the rest of the story.)

Along with the process, this book makes a strong case for what happens when such acknowledgment is provided on an ongoing basis, as well as what happens when acknowledgment is withheld or used inappropriately.

While the 30-Day Process will create happier and more productive employees, it is actually the means to a much larger end, a new outlook for the manager/company that fosters an atmosphere in which everyone thrives. The process quickly becomes self-affirming when it is understood that we cannot see in another that which does not already exist in us. In other words, the resulting exhilaration is felt as much by the one giving the compliments as by the one receiving them.

This book also explores the domino effect that occurs: one person, appropriately acknowledged, tends to pass the acknowledgment on, almost unconsciously, until one day the organization's employees look around and notice that something is very different. The process teaches us to think differently about the people we employ, just as Charles Plumb now thinks differently about those who packed his parachutes. In other words, the 30-Day Process, initially an end in itself, becomes the tail that wags the dog in its capacity to transform the workplace by elevating acknowledgment from a random act of appreciation to a sustained, intentional way of being.

Chapters 12 to 14 of this book profile three very different organizations that have "gotten it" with respect to the kind of acknowledgment I'm talking about. These companies understand the difference between workplace appreciation that is a *come from* rather than a *how-to*.

The idea for the 30-Day Process surfaced during a performance review in 1996. At the time I was directing the Dallas office of the Franklin Covey Company. For a long time, I have been significantly influenced by the teachings of Dr. Stephen R. Covey in his international best-seller, *The Seven Habits of Highly Effective People*. Of particular value to me has been his concept of "making deposits into the emotional bank account" of another person as a way of building trust in a relationship. Since traditional performance reviews have hardly been thought of as a way to build trust, I wondered if there was a way to blend these two ideas.

Thus, in 1996, when it was time to conduct a performance review with one of my staff, I suggested the nontraditional approach of asking if, over the course of the next thirty days, I could share with that person different things I admired and appreciated about her (which, I hoped, would be viewed as deposits into her emotional bank account). The results, as you will hear more about in the next chapter, were phenomenal.

I then tried the same process with large numbers of individuals, both inside and outside the workplace. The results were similarly impressive.

Eventually, I elected to resign my position with the Franklin Covey Company to devote myself full-time to researching and writing about what happens when organizations (and individuals) take on the task of acknowledgment in a way that produces extraordinary results.

I conducted workshops with a variety of companies to determine the outcome when people feel fully valued for their contributions. This book will expand on those results. I will examine the consequences of offering—and withholding—the kind of workplace validation we so richly deserve and desire.

In the chapters that follow, I share the significant results of what happens when individuals reconnect with their own goodness by helping another connect with his or her intrinsic qualities. I share stories about the long-term, sustainable transformation that occurs when individuals are affirmed and validated, when their gifts and skills are revealed and celebrated.

According to *Merriam-Webster's New Twentieth Century Dictionary,* one definition of acknowledgment is an "admission of the truth . . . about our true character." Thus, I am writing about the kind of acknowledgment for which most of us yearn but rarely get, that which validates our "true character." Specifically, I want to encourage each of us to do a better job—for some of us a *much* better job—of letting the people around us know how much we appreciate the qualities, skills, and competencies that make life and work a little better.

It is my hope that this book will become an indispensable tool for "breaking the good news" about ourselves.

CHAPTER TWO

ONCE UPON A PERFORMANCE REVIEW

OUTSTANDING LEADERS GO OUT OF THEIR WAY TO BOOST THE
SELF-ESTEEM OF THEIR PERSONNEL. IF PEOPLE BELIEVE IN
THEMSELVES, IT'S AMAZING WHAT THEY CAN ACCOMPLISH.
—SAM WALTON

A funny thing happened on the way to a performance review in 1996.

Like many of you, I am no stranger to performance reviews, having been on both the giving and receiving ends of this workplace ritual for many years. Also like many of you, for me it was usually a toss-up as to which was more dreaded, being the giver or the receiver. As director of the Dallas office of the Covey Leadership Center (now the Franklin Covey Company), part of my job responsibilities included annual performance reviews of the staff.

On this particular occasion in 1996, I found myself facing a unique challenge. One of the reviews I was scheduled to conduct was with our senior client coordinator, Kelly Newman, who also happened to be my daughter. As her "boss," I could *maybe* concede that there was room for *some* performance improvement in one or two *minor* areas. As her mother, however, I was convinced that there was *no* area where improvement was needed since she was, after all, perfect.

Unable to reconcile these seemingly competing inner directives, I resorted to that most human and inane of behaviors: I crossed my fingers and hoped some miracle would intervene to relieve me of the necessity of any kind of meeting that would require me to point out anything even vaguely resembling a flaw in Kelly's job performance. I prayed that Kelly would, *on her own,* somehow discern areas in which she could improve her performance and transform herself accordingly and immediately. Such action on her part would not only validate my belief about her perfection, it would eliminate any responsibility from my end for going ahead with the required performance review.

I still had my fingers crossed when the designated date and time for the performance review arrived. I was confident that Kelly would show up with a ready-made list of areas for performance improvement that *she* had discerned and that she would say something like "Mom, I've taken the liberty of reviewing myself in advance of our meeting. Here are some areas for improvement I've discerned, along with some suggestions on how I might achieve a new level of performance."

My role would then be limited to saying "Thanks for sharing," and our meeting would be concluded.

It didn't happen that way.

When Kelly showed up for our meeting, she sat quietly and expectantly. Eventually I opened my mouth to begin. I found "another voice" taking over for my own, and it spoke these words:

"Kelly, would it be okay if once a day for the next thirty days I shared a different quality or trait that I admire and appreciate about you?"

The five seconds of silence that followed seemed interminable. Finally, Kelly recovered first and said, "Sure, when do we begin?" I suggested we start the following day, and our "performance review" was over.

After Kelly left my office, I sat and pondered what had just happened. I theorized that the thirty-day part must have come from the belief shared by many researchers that it takes thirty days for something to become a habit, although I wasn't clear at the time that what I proposed would have any habit-forming consequences. As for coming up with thirty qualities that I admired about Kelly, that seemed an easy enough task, since she had been a cherished daughter for twenty-seven years and I considered us to have a good relationship.

What all of this had to do with a performance review was still a mystery to me. I figured that sooner or later I would need to return to that task in its more traditional form. In the meantime, I had this "other" task to complete.

When Kelly appeared in my office the next day to begin what I now refer to as the "30-Day Process," I shared a quality that I enjoyed about her, offering an example of when I had seen that characteristic displayed in her behavior. For example, one of the things I appreciate most about Kelly is her loyalty to her friends, regardless of the separation that time and geography sometimes impose. As a result of intentional efforts on her part, Kelly has remained connected with friends and neighbors who go back to her early childhood. Thus, "loyalty to friends" was one of the first attributes I shared with her.

For the next two weeks, I had no difficulty in coming up with qualities and traits that I admire about Kelly, and we both seemed to welcome our daily time together for this purpose.

Then a quite unexpected and potentially devastating fear surfaced. Although I had promised to deliver thirty traits, we were only two weeks into the process and I had already "used up" my mental list of obvious and generic qualities, those that more often than not resemble those in the Boy Scout oath: friendly, loyal, helpful, and so on. With sixteen days left to go, where was I to find the remaining traits?

Feeling inwardly embarrassed that I was having to grope for more traits to share with this extraordinary young woman, I came to the realization that it was not her good qualities that were in short supply. Rather, it was the absence of 20/20 vision on my part as far as seeing those qualities was concerned. I had become lazy and careless in allowing a few of her virtues to dominate my consciousness, losing touch with anything much deeper than the obvious.

What happened next, it turned out, eventually became the impetus to write this book.

I started observing Kelly in a way that I had not done in a long time. I paid very close attention to her actions and behaviors, particularly how she related to others. I realized that who she was for her dad was distinct from who she was for her mother, which was distinct from who she was for her sister, spouse, grandparents, cousins, and others. All of a sudden, what might have been a casually offered generic-sounding trait such as "contributing family member" now became five or six traits as I reflected on the unique qualities Kelly brought to her relationships with each of these people. Many specific examples came easily to mind as well.

Intrigued with this process of reflection and observation, I became excited about what else I might discover about Kelly. The more I observed and reflected, the more I saw, and the more I saw, the more there was to share.

At the end of thirty days, we ended the process, although at that point I could easily have kept going.

In the days that followed, I realized that several significant things had occurred, not the least of which was a greatly expanded paradigm of who Kelly was—and is—for me. I saw her in a whole new light. She was so much more than I had ever given her credit for being, and none of it was hidden. It was there in all its beauty just waiting for an observer to see it.

There was another significant development as a result of this thirty-day effort: Kelly's work performance reached new levels. Already good with customers on the phone, she now became superb. She earned the kind of trust from her customers to which many in her position can only aspire. Clients who did not know the nature of my relationship with Kelly would call me to express their appreciation for the care and attention she had given their requests. (While I heard these offerings from the perspective of a very pleased boss, I heard them even more clearly from the perspective of a very proud mother.)

I believe that what happened during those thirty days that shifted Kelly's performance was an expanded perception of herself. When people have the opportunity to reconnect with the qualities that make them valuable to others, they start to behave like people who are valued and appreciated. They exhibit a confidence grounded in self-worth that quickly translates into higher productivity.

Of even greater value is what happens to the quality and depth of a relationship when two people understand and acknowledge what they admire and appreciate about each other.

Industrial psychologists have been quick to confirm this phenomenon, and much has been written about what happens to productivity and performance when employees are given a positive vision of themselves. We have long known that when we feel good about ourselves, it is reflected in our behavior with others, both at home and at work.

While Kelly's work performance improved and my paradigm of her greatly expanded, she had her own reaction to those thirty days we spent together:

When my mom approached me with the idea of offering me a trait a day for thirty days, I was intrigued. I was pregnant with my first child, and this was an exciting (and anxiety-provoking) time in my life. The 30-Day Process became a calming routine. The process increased my self-awareness and boosted my self-esteem. I look at myself differently now, and I look at my relationships with others in a new light.

The process also improved and increased my communication with my mom. I thought because I saw or talked to someone regularly (even every day) that I therefore "communicated" with them regularly. The process taught me that this was not the case. For most of the thirty days, my mom and I had face-to-face communication. We were really talking and listening to each other. It was not just a passive transfer of information but a very personal connection.

Perhaps the most surprising outcome of doing this process with Kelly was its self-affirming nature. I found myself wanting to see more in *me* those qualities I admired in Kelly. There's something about acknowledging the truth about another person that has an awakening effect for the one sharing. In many ways, Kelly mirrored some of my own qualities, qualities that perhaps had become rusty over time but nonetheless were there.

Touched by what had happened to my relationship with Kelly and impressed with her new and improved work performance, I began to wonder if the 30-Day Process had been unique to us, or whether any two persons with similar intentions could achieve similar results.

Curious to find out, I asked my other daughter, Rebecca (who did not work with me), if we could do the process together. This time it would not be in the context of a performance review. It would just be me sharing with Rebecca the qualities I admired about her. She concurred, and, as with Kelly, it had a transforming and sustaining impact on the nature and quality of our relationship.

I might add that I hit the same wall midway through the process, when I seemingly ran out of the more obvious and easy-to-observe qualities. Breaking through to a new level of "seeing" the other person seems to be a critical factor in the transforming nature of the process. As with Kelly, my already good relationship with Rebecca was deepened and strengthened. (In Chapter 7 you will hear more about Rebecca's impact on my life.)

Feeling confident about these two successes, I then did the 30-Day Process with my husband, my mother, friends, other work colleagues, and so on.

By this time, the process seemed to confirm three predictable outcomes:

1. I came to have an enriched appreciation for what these people contribute to my life.
2. The person on the receiving end reconnected with his or her intrinsic goodness and the impact it has on his or her relationships with others.
3. The process left me with a deeper awareness and appreciation of my own qualities; in other words, it was self-affirming.

In my eagerness to test the process on an expanded basis, I invited others to try it with someone special, at work or at home, and provide me with feedback so I could begin to validate the accuracy of the results I had experienced. I drafted a fairly basic set of guidelines, along with a feedback form (for the giver as well as the receiver), and started my search for people who would agree to tackle what I now called the "30-Day Process."

Over the next two years, hundreds of friends, work colleagues, family members, and people at large agreed to identify a person with whom they had a key relationship and specify thirty qualities that they admired or appreciated about that person.

Much of what they shared validated my own experience. Using the feedback offered by these research participants, both givers and receivers, the 30-Day Process has been revisited, refined, and tested in a wide variety of settings, both at work and at home.

As the next chapters reveal, what started out as a mother's way of avoiding the more traditional approach to a performance review turned out to be a refreshing way to begin the delightful task of recognizing the achievements of those who give meaning and quality to our lives.

By the way, remember at the beginning of this chapter, when I said that sooner or later I would need to return to the more traditional version of a performance review with Kelly? Well, I didn't.

It wasn't necessary.

CHAPTER THREE

THE HIGH COST OF LOW TRUST

THERE ARE TWO KINDS OF ORGANIZATIONS: THOSE WHERE
PEOPLE COUNT AND THOSE WHERE PEOPLE DON'T COUNT.
—BILL GUILLORY, PH.D., *SPIRITUALITY IN THE WORKPLACE*

For many years, employees have been telling managers that when they don't feel valued for their contributions through appropriate acknowledgment, their trust in their organization erodes. When management doesn't give credit where credit is due, it's reflected in lower productivity and diminished morale, with resignation replacing passion and workplace exodus replacing workplace loyalty.

A *Wall Street Journal* article in June 2000 stated that management experts "pretty much agree that trust in the workplace has been eroding since the 1980's, largely due to the accelerating pace of change." Watson Wyatt Worldwide in Bethesda, Maryland, found in its 1999 study of 7,500 employees that only half trusted their senior managers. It also found a correlation between trust and profit: companies in which the employees trusted the top executives posted average shareholder returns 42 percentage points higher than companies where distrust was the rule.

One of the highest costs of low trust is seen in high employee turnover rates. When employees question whether or not they can trust management to value their contributions, they are quick to flee their jobs in search of greener, more affirming pastures.

The opposite is also true. When an organization proves itself to be trustworthy in providing a climate of respect for the individual, prospective employees show up in large numbers.

The Reinas, organizational development consultants in Stowe, Vermont, tell of a manufacturing plant in a small New England town that had to lay off 100 of 420 employees. It held meetings to share information. Managers hung out on the shop floor on all three shifts to answer employees' questions and to listen to their worries. They also set up outplacement centers and invited other employers to the plant to meet their people. Not surprisingly, when jobs at the plant again opened up, more than 80 percent of the laid-off workers came back.

When word gets out that an employer is committed to a working environment that honors those whom it employs, attracting and retaining high-quality performers is not an issue. When *Fortune* magazine announces its annual list of the "100 Best Companies to Work For," organizations that make the list are bombarded with applications for employment, forcing some companies to restructure their hiring procedures just to accommodate the overwhelming response.

Link that to what happens each year when *Working Mother* magazine announces its list of companies that do the best job of honoring the needs of families. A publicly held company on the list can experience an average rise of 5 to 7 percent in its stock price the day following the announcement.

Each time Dallas-based Southwest Airlines, long noted for honoring those whom it employs, announces that it is hiring pilots, it is inundated with résumés, many from senior pilots with other airlines, who readily agree to salary cuts and reduced seniority in exchange for working in an environment where their services are valued and celebrated.

The message seems to be obvious: When employees feel valued and trusted, they work harder and stay longer. When they do not, they underperform and eventually leave.

The *Wall Street Journal* article goes on to say, "Now that it's gone, many workplace experts are waking up to how important trust is, especially in a tight labor market." Research by the AON Loyalty Institute shows that trust is such a basic requirement that without it, a company's other benefits and programs don't raise employees' commitment very much.

Even so, many organizations erroneously conclude that improved benefit packages will resolve this unnecessary and voluntary flight from the workplace. But even the organizations that pride themselves on offering exceptional benefit packages are finding out that benefits in and of themselves are insufficient to retain employees. As one shrewd human resource manager put it, "Organizations need to understand that benefits are important for attracting workers, but it is an affirming culture that retains them." In one survey conducted by the University of Maryland, employees were asked to rank the ten things they wanted most in the workplace. Appreciation was ranked number one. Benefits ranked third.

The inability of benefits alone to ensure loyalty seems to be as noticeable at higher levels as it is among the rank and file. According to a survey conducted by two researchers at the University of Texas at Dallas School of Management, extensive bonuses, seven-figure salaries, and stock options don't automatically ensure chief executive officers' loyalty. The study revealed that "compensation packages do little or nothing to help corporations retain their top officers." Their study refutes the argument that companies frequently use to rationalize their high CEO compensation packages as tools to retain managerial talent: the highest-paid CEOs were as likely to change jobs as those who were paid less.

With unemployment at a twenty-five-year low, employers are searching for ways to rise above their competitors. *Business Week,* one of several magazines that now publish an annual list of the best places to work, said that in the surveys it conducts with Boston College's Center for Work and the Family, benefits are not the most critical criteria. It cited respect for employees as more important than most of the more innovative programs. When *Fortune* magazine created its highly competitive list called "The 100 Best Companies to Work For in America," it learned that while benefits play a big part in how companies are rated, what distinguishes the very best is "the kind of relationship management has with employees. Trust and respect are critical to great workplaces."

The first company to be named number one on *Fortune*'s list in 1998 was Southwest Airlines. Southwest operates on the theory that rather than depending on "canned" workplace programs, they "give employees the freedom to make a contribution." Southwest Airlines believes that all employees should know that they make a difference to the company, and it interacts with them accordingly. That this philosophy works is evidenced by the fact that at Southwest Airlines there are pilots who willingly help clean planes, gate agents who drive passengers to hospitals, gate agents who fly with anxious passengers, and executives who load baggage and pass out peanuts on flights.

Ask yourself if at your organization people feel sufficiently valued to demonstrate an equivalent kind of loyalty.

In the March 1998 issue of *HR Magazine,* First Tennessee Bank's Pat Brown, vice president and manager of family matters, shared how the bank puts numbers to its work-family success story. The bank is one of very few organizations that have been listed by *Working Mother, Business Week,* and *Fortune* magazines as a highly desirable place to work. Here's what *IIR Magazine,* quoting Pat Brown, reported:

> *"By surveying employees and customers at each bank location and analyzing the financial performance of each branch, we found that employees whose needs are met provide more value to customers. And customers satisfied with the service or product will stay with the company. In fact, business units run by managers who rank highest in the work and family area have a seven percent higher customer retention rate than other managers. This may not seem like a lot, but it amounts to millions of dollars.*
>
> *"Employees with supportive bosses stay employed at the bank 50 percent longer than other employees. By*

encouraging this supportive behavior, the bank saved more than $1 million in turnover costs in the past three years. We now have one of the highest customer retention rates of any bank in the country."

When reduced-time work with full benefits was instituted, 85 percent of the employees who switched over from full-time hours said they would have quit otherwise. The bank estimates that the total replacement costs saved have been $5,000 to $10,000 per nonmanagerial employee and $30,000 to $50,000 per executive.

The account-processing department has instituted longer shifts at the beginning of the month because that is considered a "crunch" period. Employees then take a day off during a slower time of the month. Result: the time it takes to reconcile customer accounts was reduced from ten days to four, thereby increasing customer satisfaction without increasing salary costs.

It's hard to argue with the results First Tennessee Bank gets by respecting and acknowledging its employees.

Another prominent banker, Walter Shipley, is the chairman of the Chase Manhattan Corporation. Writing in their book, *Lessons from the Top,* Thomas J. Neff and James M. Citrin quote Shipley as saying, "If people feel valued, you have a much stronger company." Shipley acts as if the people who work at Chase make the difference. He said, "When we bought Texas Commerce Bank, I always referred to it as a merger, even though we were three times their size and even though we bought them. If people feel valued and feel that they are being treated fairly, we will have a much more powerful company."

BNA, a publisher based in Washington, D.C., also appeared on all three lists of the best places to work. Tony Harris, its director of diversity and employee relations, says that employment candidates love to hear about the recognition BNA receives and says it's also a great morale booster for existing employees.

What employers who make these best-places-to-work lists are telling us is that it makes good business sense to honor and acknowledge the needs of their employees. Corporate stakeholders are beginning to realize that worklife programs can help boost employee satisfaction, which translates into happier customers and increased profits.

Jan Belcher is a close friend of mine who works as a personal coach with individuals in organizations to improve their effectiveness. Sometimes the marginal performance of those she is asked to coach is less a result of incompetence than it is of not feeling valued or secure in what they are being asked to do. Jan described such an encounter with a woman she was hired to coach.

This young woman was promoted to a supervisory position. Two of the people she supervised were much older than she was and had a tendency to make life difficult for their new, and much younger, boss. Add to this the fact that she was intimidated by her own boss, and you have an employee just waiting to fail. During one of their coaching sessions, Jan asked the young woman how she felt about being singled out as "someone worth keeping; someone in whom the company was willing to invest time and money to ensure her success; someone worthy of being coached."

The newly promoted supervisor responded, "It feels

great. It feels like I really matter." When asked when the last time she had felt acknowledged for her contribution had been, the young woman said she could not recall a single time in her life when anyone had taken the time to tell her they valued what she did.

Sometimes a modest investment by an organization in something as cost-effective as personal coaching can be a catalyst for improved performance, not because an employee's skills are enhanced but because *the employee now has a new level of trust in an organization that values his or her efforts.*

A word of caution: One incident of providing validation to employees doesn't turn around an individual or an organization. It is the ability to provide sustaining, intentional recognition for what others bring to the table that impacts who we are and how we perform.

In some larger organizations, acknowledgment is often limited to well-intentioned—and very expensive—reward and recognition programs. No amount of money is spared in lavish annual award banquets to honor designated employees, offering extravagant paid vacations, expensive gifts, and a handshake from the president. While there is nothing wrong with setting aside time to honor the contributions of employees in a formalized fashion, it should never be a substitute for ongoing, sustained validation.

I know of one organization that had "employee of the month" awards for a wide category of jobs. Early each year a Presidential Awards Banquet was held to honor all of the previous year's recipients of these monthly awards. This meant that if someone was named the "March Employee of the Month" in a given job category, he or she was not formally acknowledged for that recognition until the Presidential Awards Banquet the following year. Absent any intervening acknowledgment on a more regular basis, recognition at the banquet felt empty and meaningless. There was one year when several employees boycotted the annual awards banquet for this very reason. They said the acknowledgment was "too little, too late."

In other words, the amount of money spent on reward and recognition programs does not always equal the value created. In fact, the opposite can sometimes be true. Consider this much more cost-effective example.

In the late 1980s, I was working as a consultant with a large wholesale grocery distribution center in the Toronto area of Canada. The director of this operation was a kind-hearted man who ran the company's warehouse and was frequently cited for his contribution to the bottom line. Between his office and the warehouse itself, there was an area in which about twenty data-entry clerks worked, tracking inventory, entering orders, and performing other administrative tasks.

Sensing that this group's productivity was falling off, the warehouse manager ordered a morale survey. He was not surprised when the survey results confirmed his suspicions about low morale but was devastated when the survey results pointed to him as the culprit. From his perspective, he ran an efficient warehouse whose profits were used to guarantee the salary and benefits of the very people who were now blaming him for their low morale.

To his credit, he went to this group of employees and asked what he could do to improve his relationship with them. They told him that while he ran the warehouse very well, he seemed to care little about them personally and who they were as individuals. They added that they also did not feel acknowledged for the role *they* played in the successful operation of the warehouse.

His solution was simple and inexpensive. Using a blank legal pad, he wrote the names of all the employees down the left-hand side of the page. Across the top he listed the days of the workweek. His goal was to say something personal every day to each of these employees and enter a check mark by each name when he had done so.

Most important, he told his employees of his intentions.

This kind of recognition not being a habit, he realized at 4:30 P.M. on the first day of this effort that the group would be leaving at 5:00 P.M. and he had yet to say anything personal to a single person. Feeling sheepish and embarrassed, he nonetheless went out to the area where they worked and hastily made his rounds, asking some their names, asking others about their children and still others about their outside interests. In each instance, he thanked the employee for his or her contribution to the warehouse.

Vowing not to make the same mistake twice, the next day he was able to complete his "acknowledgment" rounds by midafternoon. Each day the task became easier and more natural. By the end of two weeks, he threw away the legal pad because daily acknowledgment of and interaction with the employees had become a habit. Not surprisingly, when another morale survey was conducted six months later, he received the highest marks possible as a manager, and productivity was up by 20 percent! All this for the cost of a legal pad and some intentional time spent with his team of people.

Let's face it, for the most part, workplace feedback that is intentional and deliberate is usually in the form of an occasional performance review that focuses almost exclusively on job areas where weaknesses are perceived. These reviews rarely address the qualities for which we yearn to be affirmed, the things that represent who we *are* rather than what we *do*.

Some less enlightened organizations even go so far as to tell their managers to withhold praise, fearing that it will make employees complacent.

Even worse are the companies that make a feeble stab at acknowledgment without examining the consequences of their actions.

An example of this occurred when an organization noted for promoting teamwork decided one year that everyone would participate in the annual bonus pool, regardless of rank or role. This meant that administrative and clerical staff would participate for the first time in the distribution of annual bonuses. Percentages of the bonus pool were assigned for each job level, *without calculating what this translated into in terms of actual dollars and cents.* As a result, some clerical staff received a bonus check of $27 while senior managers received much heftier amounts.

One of the recipients of a $27 bonus check said she felt insulted, not acknowledged. She further stated that she was considering mailing the check back to management, telling them that they obviously needed this money more than she did. What started out as a gesture of acknowledgment was not thought through and wound up costing the company the loyalty of many of its employees.

A similar outcome was thwarted by a savvy division director of a large state agency in Texas. Her division of 110 people was allotted three merit awards annually, meaning a 3.4 percent salary raise for the lucky three. Her concern was for the other 107, many of whom were equally deserving.

Add to this frustration the fact that her division works very hard on a very limited budget from the state legislature. "We've done a good job of showing the legislature that we can work miracles with nothing." Their reward? The next year the legislature gave them less!

To counter what seems like incredible odds, this division director spends much of her time making her people feel personally appreciated. She has a "brag board" where she posts "good job" letters from constituents. She also sends e-mail acknowledgments when her people do a good job or receive praise for their efforts from others. She works consistently and intentionally to improve communications with her field staff. As a result of these efforts, the turnover rate in her division is about 10 percent, considerably less than her counterparts in other state agencies experience.

What these examples point to is the fact that there is a direct correlation between an affirming culture and the bottom line. Companies that label acknowledgment "soft" or "too time-consuming" may need to rethink their positions.

One executive I interviewed said his company had a turnover rate of 150 percent *a year*, about 1,600 jobs, at a cost of approximately $2.5 million. When exiting employees were polled regarding their reasons for leaving, the number one reason given was that they did not feel valued for the work they did. The number two reason cited was low pay.

The company scrambled to come up with higher pay but did nothing about introducing a system of acknowledgment. The result? Turnover *increased*, with job vacancies averaging about 1,700 in 1999.

As part of this book's research, I developed and delivered "acknowledgment workshops" for a wide variety of organizations. I wanted to validate the relationship between acknowledgment and the bottom line. Participants in these workshops were asked to identify both the "hard" and "soft" costs to the organization when some sort of ongoing positive feedback was not offered. The responses always included such things as high turnover, low morale, poor communication, higher absenteeism, little or no loyalty, low productivity, me-versus-we thinking, backstabbing, lying, deception, and so on.

When these conditions are present in an organization, they affect not only those who are employed by the company but customers, vendors, and other constituents as well. If employees do not feel valued for what they do, they are less inclined to provide the kind of service and productivity that ensure a company a healthy bottom line.

For example, a major airline with a history of labor-management problems cited one union with which its annual arbitration costs alone exceeded $2 million. Eventually it was discovered that the reason so many grievances with union members went directly to arbitration was that members bypassed the much less costly grievance procedure, which they were contractually allowed to do. When I asked why the grievance procedure was bypassed, the union members responded that they did not trust management to resolve their issues at that level. When I asked why they didn't trust management, their response was that they didn't feel appreciated by their first-level supervisors. Employees' failure to feel appreciated for their contributions resulted in expensive and sometimes unnecessary settlements.

Contrast this example with that of Southwest Airlines, which boasts excellent relationships with its unions. In January 1995, in a move unprecedented in aviation history, Southwest pilots signed a ten-year contract with the company. Not only was the duration of the contract unheard of, but the pilots further agreed to freeze their wages for the first five years in exchange for stock options. Company officials said that the high level of trust between the airline and its unions made such a move possible.

While much has been written about Southwest Airlines and the extraordinary lengths to which it goes to validate, celebrate, and acknowledge its employees, it is newsworthy because Southwest is the exception and not the rule. As far as acknowledgment is concerned, most organizations still seem to be stuck in their own version of insanity, doing what they've always done and, sadly, getting what they've always got. It is the reason, I suspect, why the phrase we have created for disgruntled post office employees, "going postal," has become synonymous with a disgruntled employee who vows to get a company's attention.

Why have we not adopted a similar phrase to describe a workplace to which employees are delighted to come to work each day?

In the workshops I conduct, participants are also asked to describe the payoffs of working in an environment where praise and acknowledgment are an ongoing part of the culture. Not surprisingly, they speak of lower employee turnover, higher trust, increased productivity, open and honest communication, greater loyalty to the organization, a we-versus-me mind-set, less absenteeism, and an overall sense of well-being. Again, each of these resulted in reduced costs and increased revenues.

The challenge is neither hidden nor complicated. What is needed is a resource, a tool, that supports enlightened employers in building trust . . . one relationship at a time. That's what the 30-Day Process is designed to do.

Let's take an up-close, personal view of this process.

CHAPTER FOUR

A THIRTY-DAY JOURNEY THAT LASTS A LIFETIME

I CAN LIVE A LONG TIME ON A GOOD COMPLIMENT.
—MARK TWAIN

I have referred several times to the 30-Day Process created in 1996 during Kelly's performance review. Thanks to the feedback from everyone who was a part of the research for this book, the process has been refined and improved. As a result, to those of you who choose to do the 30-Day Process and follow the guidelines offered in this chapter, I can promise the following:

- Your skill at and capacity for *habitually* acknowledging others will be greatly enhanced.
- You will transform the depth and quality of the relationships you feel are most important.
- Workplace performance will significantly improve as a culture of acknowledgment emerges.

The 30-Day Process, simply stated, is this:

*Once a day, for thirty days, share with someone whose rela-
tionship is important to you a different quality or trait that you
admire, appreciate, or value about that person.*

Although simple enough in its premise, the process pres-
ents some unexpected challenges and for many requires an
unaccustomed level of commitment. In fact, for some of you
the biggest challenge may be your willingness to tackle *anything* consistently for thirty days.

Let's begin by addressing the question "Why thirty
days?"

During my years with the Franklin Covey Company, I
heard Stephen Covey say on many occasions that it generally
takes about thirty days of practice for something to become
a habit. Since the purpose of this book is to cultivate the
habit of acknowledgment, thirty days seemed reasonable.
After all, this book was prompted by what had happened
when I shared thirty traits with Kelly during our performance review experience several years ago.

Many who assisted in the research for this book mentioned that coming up with thirty traits over thirty days had
been a real stretch for them. On the other hand, asking people
to name only five or ten traits diminished the value of the
process since most of us can hold our breath and think of five
or ten qualities we appreciate about those with whom our relationship is important. It is also likely that those off-the-top-of-
your-head traits are already known to the other person. In
order for acknowledgment to become a habit, you will have to
stretch yourself, as I was required to do with Kelly once I had
exhausted my list of "Boy Scout oath" qualities. It is this act of

purposefully expanding our vision that allows us to move from the obvious to a much deeper level of appreciation for those who contribute so richly to our lives.

I know that for some of you, committing to anything for thirty days is a stretch, whether it's an exercise program, eliminating sugar from your diet, enforcing a promise not to gossip, showing up on time, etc. As with all these efforts, the eager excitement with which we begin starts to wane when the going gets a little tough. Making something a habit requires you to move beyond the desire to delay or quit. It is jumping this hurdle that creates a breakthrough in the depth and quality of the relationship you have with the person with whom you are sharing.

With that in mind, the following guidelines are offered to increase your success with the 30-Day Process, which elevates recognition from a random pat on the back to a sustaining celebration of those who matter most to you.

30-DAY PROCESS GUIDELINES

1. If you start the process, be committed to finishing it.

I remember reading some years ago a definition of sainthood that stated: "Saints are people who keep their word." My initial response was one of confusion, since I presumed that most people intend to keep their word and yet there are so few saints. Then I got it: while many of us *intend* to keep our word, few of us actually do it. Hence, there are lots of good intentions but very few saints among us.

Almost everyone who participates in the 30-Day Process starts out with a high degree of enthusiasm and optimism and a clear commitment to stay the course. It is not uncommon, when I introduce this process to potential participants, to hear responses such as "Wow, this is something I have always been meaning to do . . . now I have a format for doing it!" "Let's get started!" "How do I begin?"

As with many of our other good intentions, the excitement about a promise to deliver thirty traits can wane when schedules conflict, unforeseen events (such as illness) crop up, or other matters competing for your attention suddenly seem more important. Any of these can result in an unintended but nonetheless premature death of the process. Can you imagine what happens to your partner when a promise to deliver thirty qualities is abandoned after you share only seven or eight? You're right. The initial enthusiasm and anticipation felt by your partner is replaced with a confirmation of his or her worst suspicion, namely that "there probably aren't thirty things to admire about me after all."

Quitting in the middle of the process has an eroding and demoralizing impact on the relationship.

I urge you to weigh your level of commitment carefully before beginning the process. If you are unsure that you can complete thirty traits, you may want to begin by promising to deliver five traits, then extend that to another five, and so on, until you have shared thirty traits. This allows the more gradual development of your acknowledgment muscles, which may have atrophied through lack of use!

2. Share the traits in person.

The first time you do this process, select someone whom you can arrange to see daily or regularly so each trait can be shared in person. The feedback from those who have tried this process overwhelmingly confirms the greater value of sharing face-to-face. While you may occasionally elect to share a trait by phone, the impact is stronger and takes on a deeper quality for both persons when it is done in person.

Having stated this preference, I can also tell you that some people have successfully completed the 30-Day Process, *because of special circumstances,* over the phone, via written correspondence, or, in the case of my husband, by e-mail with his son, who was an army captain based in South Korea. Clearly the geographic distance, schedule, and accessibility of the other person will determine whether you do this process in person or select another method of communicating.

Note: E-mail should *not* be your method of choice for sharing traits with your partner! There may be occasional exceptional circumstances that warrant it, but they should be just that—exceptional.

When attempting the 30-Day Process for the first time, I strongly recommend you select someone whom you can arrange to see regularly, with the intention that most or all of the sharing will be done in person. Once you have some success with the process, you may want to try it with someone whose schedule or location justifies a method of sharing where face-to-face contact is limited or difficult.

3. The partner you select should be the partner **you** *select.*

This guideline sounds like a blinding flash of the obvious. After all, who knows better than you the relationships you value? Of course you would be the person to choose your partner for this process. As obvious as this guideline may sound, there have been organizations where a decision was made to have a team of people try the process simultaneously and where choosing a partner was *not* voluntary. The results were mixed at best.

In one company, for example, a division head wanted her staff to do the process together and decided to have each person draw the name of his or her partner from a basket containing slips of paper with everyone's name. As a result, several people drew the name of someone about whom they had mixed feelings or, in some instances, toward whom they felt downright hostile. To make matters worse, employees were told that if they did not complete the thirty-day sharing assignment, it would be reflected in their personnel files. Not surprisingly, the feedback forms collected from these people reported that their relationship with their partner actually worsened because, as one participant stated, "the process felt forced and unnatural, and the traits sounded more like hypocrisy than sincerity."

In another organization, the leader of an intact work team whose heart was in the right place (he had actually obtained prior approval from everyone about participating in such a process) nonetheless chose to assign partners rather than letting the choice be voluntary. In this instance, people who were trying the process for the first time felt robbed of an opportunity to share with someone at work for whom they had great respect and admiration.

Contrast these results with those achieved by the Walk the Talk Company in Dallas, Texas, an organization that provides training and publications to many businesses. Eric Harvey, the president of this company (and a good friend of mine), received enthusiastic support from his staff about trying out the 30-Day Process. He allowed the staff to choose their partners, and the results were significantly different from those of the two companies mentioned above. One hundred percent of the employees participated, and all of them completed the process. Their feedback, to a person, was enthusiastic and affirming, and spoke warmly of relationships deepened, including an expanded vision of themselves as seen through the eyes of another.

Because this process should *always* be a voluntary initiative, selecting a partner should *always* be a personal choice.

4. Choose a partner with whom you have a healthy relationship.

When you do the 30-Day Process, choose a relationship that is emotionally healthy and stable, a good relationship that you want to make better. This might be with a key coworker, a family member, or a friend. Trying the process with a partner with whom your relationship is strained or unstable diminishes your chances of succeeding. Any misgivings you have about this person will conflict with your desire to offer acknowledgment.

I found this out the hard way when I promised to share thirty traits with someone whom I did not respect and whose values were often at odds with my own. However, because our relationship was important to me at the time, I figured I was mature enough to complete the process with him, in the hope that by finding thirty positive qualities in this person I might shift my opinion of him. Not only did this not happen (it turned out that I was not the emotionally mature person I deemed myself to be), but, to my embarrassment, I begged out of the commitment about ten days into the process because I couldn't overcome my objections to and resentful feelings about this person.

I share this story to emphasize my belief that the process works best when you are sharing with someone whom you already admire, respect, and enjoy.

The process is not designed to be a therapeutic approach to "fixing" a strained relationship. It is designed to encourage you to shift from *thinking* good things about another person to intentionally and openly *sharing* them.

Remember, the 30-Day Process has as its purpose developing the *habit* of acknowledgment. My goal is not to have you do the process with everyone you know but rather to try it with one or more people until the habit is firmly in place. Then the habit will take over and everyone in the workplace will benefit when the resulting culture of ongoing recognition emerges.

5. *Tell your partner what you are doing!*

Please let your partner know what you're doing. Be up front and tell your partner you would like to spend the next thirty or so days sharing qualities and traits that you admire and appreciate about him or her. Over and over again in the workshops I conduct on the 30-Day Process, the question arises: "Can I just start doing the process without telling my partner what I'm doing—you know, sort of let it be a sur-prise?" The answer is an unequivocal no.

In spite of this admonition, there have been some partici-pants who insisted on doing the process without letting their partner know in advance what was happening. Let's face it, most of us are not accustomed to giving—or receiving—the kind of sustained acknowledgment the 30-Day Process pro-vides. Therefore, it is essential to be straightforward with the person you select as your partner. Attempting to "spring" the process on someone with no advance preparation only serves to make that person highly suspicious of this "new affirming you." It's like a spouse who uncharacteristically comes home with flowers and a card "for no special reason." Rather than being flattered, his or her partner immediately becomes suspi-cious and starts trying to figure out what's *really* going on. The same is true when you attempt the 30-Day Process without let-ting your partner know your intention.

Your initial conversation with the partner you select might go something like this: "I'm working on doing a better job of letting people who are important to me know how much I appreciate their contributions [to our workplace, our family, our community, this friendship, whatever]. Since you are one of those persons for me, would it be all right if once a day, over the next thirty days, I share a different qual-ity, attribute, or trait that I admire and appreciate about you?"

This is a compelling invitation that few people, if any, will decline. That is all the more reason to be up front with your partner and let him or her know exactly what you are proposing.

6. *Learn to deal with your partner's response.*

When I extend the invitation to share thirty traits, either with an individual or in front of the room at a seminar, there is often a pause before I get a response, mostly because our brain is doing its best to convince us there must be some mistake. "Surely you don't mean *me*?" "There's no way someone could find thirty things to admire or appreciate about me!"

I remember posing this question to a group of participants from a large state agency in Texas, and their collective response was that I could probably get the job done in two or three traits since surely it would be impossible to find many more. While their response was good-natured in its tone, it nonetheless is what often happens when we face the opportunity to hear our goodness affirmed by another person on a consistent, ongoing basis.

Andy Lawrence and Eric Jackson conduct a life management seminar in Dallas called Pathways. Their belief is that affirmation is cardinal to life change. What they have learned over the years is that most people don't believe they deserve to hear good news about themselves. "People have to be taught that they deserve to hear this good news," Eric says. Andy adds, "The amount of 'plastic' persona we carry around is directly related to the degree to which we believe we don't deserve to be who we are."

Trust me when I say that almost anyone you choose as a partner for the 30-Day Process will have his or her own version of why you shouldn't or couldn't do so. One of the hardest things for your partner to do will be simply to receive the gift of your expression of appreciation.

Andy Lawrence described a "lightbulb" moment in his

life when a participant in one of his seminars told him that she had something to say to him, but before she would share it he had to promise to limit his response to "Thank you." Period. Believing that to be a reasonable, albeit unusual, request, he agreed. The participant then proceeded to share a quality she found to be extraordinary in him. "Limiting my response to those two words was one of the hardest experiences of my life." Everything in Andy wanted to discount what she had shared, believing that to do otherwise might label him as arrogant or boastful.

In truth, his willingness simply to let it soak in proved to be a turning point in his ability to give—and receive—the kind of affirming feedback *we all so richly deserve.*

Gentle coaching for your partner similar to that Andy received is good advice.

Another request to make of your partner is that he or she silence their internal conversations that may prompt him or her to say things like "That's not how I see myself" or "You must be kidding." Explain that the qualities you want to share are reflective of *your experience* of them and may or may not resonate with their own beliefs.

People completing the 30-Day Process repeatedly comment in their feedback forms that the inclination of their partners is to discount or disclaim what they are hearing. In truth, their partners were not at odds with what they were hearing; rather, they were acting out the "socially correct" acquired behavior of gently or not so gently deflecting anything good that came their way in the form of acknowledgment.

If your partner feels it necessary to say something in response to a trait you share, tell him or her that "Thank you" is sufficient. Even those of us who have a healthy curiosity about how others see us seem determined to let some skepticism surface. For example, the first time I proposed to do this process with my husband, who was very familiar with what I was doing, he couldn't resist rolling his eyes as if to say, "What good you may see is limited, and I probably already know the one or two things that are obvious."

Expect your partner to be skeptical and acknowledge this concern. Remind him or her that these are qualities you see in him or her regardless of how he or she may see or experience him- or herself.

Another tendency on the part of those receiving your input will be to tell you about all the times when they did not live up to a particular quality for which you want to acknowledge them. For example, when I told a coworker how much I appreciated her always being on time for meetings, she immediately rebutted with examples of times when she had not been punctual. When this happens, remind your partner that that kind of mind chatter is best kept silent. Once again, if your partner must say something, "Thank you" is sufficient.

Because of our social conditioning, it is tempting for your partner to want to trade acknowledgments, offering examples of when he or she has seen the same trait exhibited by you. We have been taught that it's good manners to respond to praise either by discounting it or by returning the favor. For the purposes of this process, ask your partner to let this sharing experience be limited to your insights about him or her. Let your partner know that you are always willing to hear what he or she has to say about you, but in a different setting at another time.

Be prepared, also, for the kind of thing that happened when a good friend of mine was doing the process with her longtime significant other. He found it very difficult to hear what she appreciated about him unless she was also willing to tell him something she didn't like as well. From his perspective, this provided "balance" to the sharing. My belief is that we are so undernourished in the area of getting the affirming validation we deserve that the 30-Day Process restores rather than distorts any sense of balance.

Anticipate the concerns and tendencies your partner will have when you begin this process by gently offering a structure to the dialogue that will allow your partner to move beyond his or her discomfort and become a willing recipient of what you have to share. This will allow any awkwardness about receiving feedback in such a sustained manner to quickly give way to excitement and eager anticipation.

Over and over again, participants who have been the recipients of the sharing confirmed that as the process unfolded, they become comfortable and relaxed with hearing their goodness revealed by another.

7. Make sure that only one partner shares at a time.

Sometimes participants doing the 30-Day Process ask me if the two partners can exchange traits simultaneously. This is especially true if the two partners happen to be spouses, close coworkers, or good friends. On the surface, it seems like a logical way to kill two birds with one stone: one person can share a trait with the other, and then the process can be reversed.

I recommend against doing the process this way for two reasons. First, it has a diluting effect when you are playing the role of both the one sharing and the recipient of your partner's sharing. The purpose of the process is to have the focus be exclusively on the one receiving. Second, there is a tendency to believe that all of the traits shared with the other have to be independent of any that have already been shared with you. For example, if your partner acknowledges you for the kind way in which you interact with problematic coworkers, you may respond, "Oh, no, that's what I was going to tell you tomorrow! Now I'll have to think of something else." While it is natural for both partners to share similar qualities, it is best when one partner at a time is sharing them with the other.

It is all right, at the conclusion of the 30-Day Process, to have the receiving partner choose to reverse the process and share thirty qualities with the one who has already done so. This can be done right away, or you may choose to wait a while.

8. Set a specific time for your sharing.

While the name "30-Day Process" implies that it will take place over thirty consecutive days, it is not always necessary, or sometimes even possible, for this to happen. Allow your particular circumstances to determine the regularity of your sharing. Workplace situations, for example, usually dictate that traits be offered on a Monday-through-Friday basis, skipping the weekends if it's not customary for you to see the other person outside the work environment. Others have offered the trait on an every-other-day basis because that worked best for both partners. Because my husband's son, a U.S. Army captain based in South Korea, was often in the field four days out of five, their sharing took place via e-mail once a week for an extended period of weeks. This is exceptional, but it worked for them.

Set a time of day and schedule that work best for you and your partner. Some of the most consistent feedback I have received from research participants was on the importance of agreeing *up front* on a time and place to share.

One person who elected to do the process with her boss failed to set an agreed-upon time for their daily sharing. As a result, she wondered every time she passed him in the halls if "it was the right time to share." It turned out that he was wondering the same thing, and this jockeying for the "right" time to do it ended up causing them to miss some days altogether.

While you may not always be able to meet at the agreed-upon day and time, you will save yourself a lot of hassle by determining with your partner, up front, the best time and place to do the process. For example, two friends who did the process realized that the one uninterrupted time of day both of them had available was 6:00 A.M. So every morning at six they met (at the gym) and shared a trait. Both acknowledged at the end of the process that it had been an exhilarating way to begin their day.

Others who have done the process at work have selected a time when both participants knew their paths would cross daily and set that as their time for sharing. For my husband and myself, right before going to bed was the best time for us to share.

Be mindful of the fact that circumstances may interrupt the agreed-upon day or time for sharing. If you find yourself having to skip a day, for whatever reason, communicate this to your partner. Let him or her know that something has happened (you were called out of town, had a family emergency, had a schedule change, or whatever) and renegotiate a time to resume the sharing. Failure to communicate this disruption can result in your partner wondering if you ran out of qualities to share and send him or her into a tailspin of disappointment. Remember, it's normal that your agreed-upon time for sharing may have to be altered occasionally. The key is to communicate about these exceptions and keep the integrity of the process intact.

If you find that you have indeed skipped a day of sharing, it is better not to "double up" on the qualities when the sharing resumes. Each quality deserves its own special day, even if it means extending the process an extra day or so. I learned this firsthand when I did the process with my husband, Tom. Our agreement was to share during thirty consecutive days. When our schedules prevented sharing one day, I assumed that the next day I would need to share two qualities with Tom, to make up for our lost day. He was kind enough to tell me that his preference was not to have them doubled up but rather to hear the qualities one at a time, so their meaning could sink in. Others who have shared their experiences with me have had a similar recommendation. Their preference was always to extend the process another day or two rather than double up on the sharing of traits.

In one example, a participant said that her partner had

stopped sharing qualities about halfway through their agreed-upon thirty consecutive days. Then, near the end of the thirty days, her partner had shared eleven qualities at once and declared the process complete. Needless to say, the intent and impact of the process had been diminished substantially, especially because her partner offered no explanation for the gap in sharing.

In this kind of situation, when something happens that may temporarily suspend the sharing of traits as agreed upon, I recommend that you tell your partner that while you regret the disruption, you would like to start again where you left off. This kind of integrity sends a strong message to your partner about your intentions and how you feel about the relationship.

9. Let yourself discover some of the qualities along the way.

It is not necessary—or even recommended—that you identify all thirty traits *before* you begin the process. In fact, discovering some of the qualities as you go along is a key part of the process. You may recall that it was my "hitting the wall" experience with Kelly and Rebecca that opened my eyes to a whole boatload of qualities I might not otherwise have seen. In most instances, as you move through the process, traits you hadn't noticed before will surface and you can add them to your list. For example, when I was doing the process with my daughter Kelly, one of the things I discovered about her was how much I liked the way she received and dealt with feedback, not only from me but from others as well. This was a quality I hadn't noticed or thought about before but that was quickly added to the list of characteristics I admire about her.

Note: I recommend that you keep a written list of the traits as you go along. This prevents duplication and provides a "road map" of the traits as you progress through the process.

Even the best-intentioned and most creative of us is sometimes at a loss for words when wanting to describe something that we like about another person. After all, isn't one of the main reasons we purchase greeting cards the fact that they express the very sentiment we are seeking? To facilitate your own experience with this process, I have included a glossary of the most frequently cited traits by persons completing the 30-Day Process as part of this book's research. Appendix II should be used freely to facilitate your own selection of descriptive traits. After all, our uniqueness lies not in the fact that we are, for example, kind (the most frequently cited trait), but rather how that kindness shows up from your perspective. In another appendix, I have included a sample list of thirty traits, along with a typical example of each. I have done this to give you a sense of where you're headed. You will note that all the traits can be conveyed in a single word or a short phrase.

10. Give a specific example for each trait that is shared.

Since many of us possess qualities similar to those we admire in others, it is helpful to offer an example of what *you* mean when you see that quality in your partner. For example, almost everyone who does the 30-Day Process gets around to saying to their partner that he or she is "kind." It is a quality most of us possess. However, what kindness means to me and what it means to you may be two different things. Therefore, it is helpful—and necessary—to be specific about the quality you are acknowledging another person for.

If you want to praise someone for being punctual, for example, is it because he or she always completes work assignments on time, honors a curfew at home, shows up on time for meetings? Let him or her know how and when you see this trait or behavior displayed. Since most of us want to do more of what works well, it is helpful to know exactly what it is about us that is being affirmed.

In the course of a performance review at work, a boss rarely has a problem telling an employee *specifically* what it is that he or she is doing poorly. It is just as important to tell others, with the same amount of specificity, what it is they are doing well.

Therefore, when sharing with your partner during the 30-Day Process, always give a specific example of the trait you are describing.

11. "Stuff" happens; be prepared.

It is wise to understand up front that since you will be doing the process with someone with whom you have a close relationship, things will happen that will annoy you about him or her or otherwise get in the way during your thirty days of sharing. When this happens, it is important to remember that *that person's qualities exist independently of your feelings about him or her at any point in time.* Behave with integrity when this occurs.

For example, when I was doing the process with my husband, Tom, he did something one day that was insignificant in the grand scheme of things but was nonetheless annoying, like forgetting to set the trash out. My immediate ego-driven reaction was not to share a quality with him that day (to teach him a lesson or whatever). It took courage to create a context in which the sharing could occur and be unaffected by my feelings about the other incident.

I remember an occasion when I was planning to share with a coworker the trait of punctuality. He was late for our meeting! My ego wanted to say something like "Well, I *was* going to share the quality of punctuality with you today, but apparently I was mistaken about your relationship to that trait." There will always be exceptions to even our best behaviors. When this happens, it is good to remember that the person's behavior that day was an exception, not an indictment of that person. *Who we are exists independently of our behavior at any given time or in any given place.*

In some rare instances, if you find yourself unable to share with sincerity because you're stuck with feelings of anger or annoyance, be willing to say to your partner, "This process is too important for me to share a quality when I'm harboring these feelings of resentment [or whatever]. I'd like to suspend the sharing for today and resume tomorrow, when I trust myself to be in a better mood. Would that be okay?"

Failure to provide some kind of clarification can result in your using a tone of voice that is anything but affirming.

I cannot overemphasize the likelihood that these kinds of feelings will occur during the process. If you anticipate this possibility up front, it will make honoring your commitment easier. Even discussing it with your partner before beginning the process may make such disruptions more manageable.

12. Have fun with the process.

When trying the process, especially the first time, there is a tendency to get so serious about "doing it right" that some of the fun and spontaneity are lost. Be prepared to have fun with the process. This happens when you share some of the lighter aspects of another's charm. For example, I shared with my husband that I really liked his hair. His response was "Which part, the part that's falling out or the part that's turning gray?" We both had a good laugh, and I reminded him that his hair was something I just happened to like about him.

While some of the qualities you share may be of a more serious nature, don't overlook the lighter side of what you enjoy about another.

13. Complete the process with style and grace.

When you have shared thirty traits, it is important to bring closure to the process. Closure doesn't mean that you never have to acknowledge this person again. To the contrary, you will become more conscious than ever of qualities you enjoy, admire, and appreciate about him or her. When this happens, by all means, tell that person.

When you complete the 30-Day Process, thank the other person for participating. Share with him or her any insights you may have gained about him or her, or yourself, as you went through the process. It is also all right for the other person to reciprocate with his or her own insights.

Another optional way to bring closure to the process is by presenting your partner with a permanent reminder of who he or she is for you. This might be a written list of the traits you share or a more formalized version of that person's qualities. For example, when I complete the process with an individual, I write down all of the traits I have shared, using one or two words for each trait. I then have the list reduced to credit-card size and laminated, and present it to that person as a permanent reminder of what I admire and appreciate about him or her.

A production planner with a large telecommunications company in Dallas did a version of the 30-Day Process with her boss. When the process was completed, she bought a small photo album with protective inserts inside. She then made up a page for each trait she had shared with her boss. She even added clip art pertaining to the trait for each page. In the front of the album, she included a poem about friendship, telling her boss how much she appreciated their friendship. She suggested to her boss that the album be used as a "rainy-day book" for those times when she could use a little lift—as we all can at times. The production planner added that putting the album together for her boss had been as fulfilling for her as it was enjoyed by her boss. Finally, she added that she was starting on the 30-Day Process next with her daughter and would look for an equally creative way to present a permanent reminder to her.

What did the boss think about the album? "It was one of the most thoughtful gifts I have received." The boss described herself as one who "could hardly wait for the time each day a trait was shared. It makes me feel good to think that someone thinks that highly of me and my work."

Another 30-Day Process participant wrote a letter to a coworker with whom she had shared thirty traits. In the letter, she reviewed all of the shared traits along with an example of each of those qualities as expressed by her colleague.

Some of us are very creative and enjoy activities like these. Others are not nearly so creatively inclined, and that's fine, too. I do think it's important to give at least a written list of the traits to the person so he or she can review them from time to time.

Finally, expect the relationship to be transformed. It will.

Note: I would be very interested in hearing from those of you who decide to try the 30-Day Process. You can share your results with me on my Web site, www.dottiegandy.com. I plan to write a follow-up book that will profile your experiences, so I hope you will take the time to give me the benefit of your insights.

Even when our eagerness to start the 30-Day Process seems sufficient to proceed, there are a couple of challenges that need to be addressed with respect to our real motivation for doing so. These challenges are addressed in the next chapter.

CHAPTER FIVE

THE 30-DAY PROCESS: MOTIVATION OR MANIPULATION?

THE HIGHEST COMPLIMENT LEADERS CAN RECEIVE ARE THOSE
THAT ARE GIVEN BY THE PEOPLE WHO WORK FOR THEM.
—JAMES L. BARKSDALE

Deciding to undertake the 30-Day Process represents a quantum leap in our desire to drive the corporate culture in the direction of valuing every employee for his or her contributions. This means everyone, management as well as nonmanagement. Our universal desire to be recognized for who and what we are makes no distinction by rank, tenure, or job title. All of us yearn to hear our intrinsic worth validated by those who work for us and for whom we work.

This dynamic is a tricky challenge for some who try the 30-Day Process. The challenge is in your intention. Most people use the process responsibly to impact the quality of a relationship or motivate the performance of an individual now in touch with his or her best qualities.

As with other activities, however, there are some people who approach the process with the intent to manipulate.

These are the folks who attach a "so that . . ." to their motivation. This is especially true when the process is done by a subordinate with his or her boss. The temptation to "do" the 30-Day Process *so that* you will be liked more, get a promotion, or get the transfer you've wanted is often just too tempting to resist. After all, if there's so much at stake for the one on the receiving end, should there also not be something in it for the one giving?

Actually, this is a pretty easy question to address, mainly because if your motivation is anything other than a sincere desire to appreciate the qualities of another, it's unlikely you will even complete the process. Staying with the process for thirty days requires a lot from the person choosing to do the sharing. If that person does not truly intend to let someone else know he or she is valued, the interest in sticking with it quickly fades and the task becomes onerous. When manipulators quit midway through the process, the transparency of their motives sends a clear message to their partners.

Even when their intentions are sincere and genuine, many who have done the process with a boss or superior have felt torn between a sincere desire to acknowledge and a fear that their sharing will be perceived as manipulative. As stories throughout this book attest, regardless of the boss's reaction in the beginning, if your motivation is pure, he or she will be won over long before the process ends.

It is natural for the best of us to question whether people are really being honest when they say they want to acknowledge us for *thirty* things we do well. But that's *our* limited belief about ourselves talking, not the person who has asked to do the process with us.

The 30-Day Process is a form of acknowledgment that most of us have never experienced, namely, that it has no quid pro quo. In other words, there is no "so that" attached to the outcome. Initiating the process is not done *so that* your child will like you better, your boss will come to know how really indispensable you are, your teen will start trusting you again, your spouse will finally discover what a sweet deal he or she really has, your friend will learn just how much he or she needs you, your work colleagues will see the light as far as your contributions are concerned, and so forth.

If a *so that*—no matter how cleverly disguised—is part of your motivation for doing the process, you are probably doomed before you begin. On the other hand, if your commitment, compassion, and curiosity are authentic, you can indeed expect some type of transformation. In other words, the suspension of any "so that" may actually produce the change or shift you seek. On the other hand, any manipulation on your part as far as your intentions are concerned will probably diminish rather than enhance the relationship you have with the other person.

One participant revealed that for a long time she had nagged her grown son about his physical well-being, believing him to be overweight and unhealthy. As a result of his growing resentment, the son had not phoned his mother in more than a year and a half (although she continued to call him regularly). When this mother decided to do the 30-Day Process with her son, I cautioned her about having any expectations that he would change and suddenly decide to become more committed to his physical well-being. I reminded her that while change was possible, she should not enter the process with that expectation. She assured me of the purity of her intentions and began the process. In less than a week, her *son called her* to share several things, including *his own* ideas for becoming more physically healthy. This happened because she did not have any hidden expectations. Not only did her son not see her efforts as manipulative, his self-esteem soared and he chose *for himself* to take better care of himself physically.

If the 30-Day Process is used by you as a manipulation to foster favor with another, I can almost guarantee that you will fail. Despite our belief that we can camouflage our real intentions from another, it rarely happens. In fact, if you aren't willing to do the process from a sincere desire to acknowledge another, I recommend you not do it at all.

There is one notable exception to the no "so that" rule: If a manager or an organization intends to create a culture where acknowledgment is prevalent, of course they will utilize the 30-Day Process *so that* a shift in how people relate to each other will occur. It is an intention founded on a desire to validate the efforts of those one relies on.

Another challenge presented by the kind of acknowledgment encouraged by the 30-Day Process is whether or not there is a process of selective inclusion or exclusion where choosing participants is concerned. If a manager has six direct reports, does he or she need to do the process with all of them in order to avoid hurt feelings? If so, doesn't this represent a huge and time-consuming commitment on the part of the boss? On the other hand, does selecting only one or two direct reports send the wrong message to the others?

And what about an employee who is performing marginally? Should he or she be "rewarded" with the process just like his or her colleagues who may be more stellar performers and perhaps more likable to boot?

These are both valid questions and worthy of comment. So let's look at each of them to see what options we have.

1. If I have more than a few direct reports, must I do the 30-Day Process with all of them in order to be fair?

Remember that the purpose of the 30-Day Process is to make acknowledgment a habit for *you,* the one initiating the process. For most of us, doing the process one to three times accomplishes this. Therefore, it is unnecessary to do the process with everyone who reports to you, although the goal is certainly admirable and worthy of consideration.

The key to your success when you have more than one direct report is to be candid and honest about your intentions. Tell all of them that you want to improve your skills as a caring and acknowledging boss. Let them know that all of them are worthy of this kind of boss. Then tell them about the process, saying that you want to improve your skills by trying it with one or two of them. To avoid any appearance of favoritism with respect to who is selected, perhaps random drawing of a name or names in the presence of all of them would ensure fairness. *At the same time, introduce the process to them and invite them to try it with one another as well.* This will accelerate your goal of impacting the work environment, even if only one or two others elect to begin the process with a coworker.

As far as the time commitment is concerned, when electing to do the process with several direct reports, you can read in Chapter 9 how one hospital director shared traits with her direct reports, many of whom worked on shifts different from her own.

2. What about the marginal employees?

As simplistic as this response may sound, it is precisely those employees who are deserving of your time and attention where the 30-Day Process is concerned. Marginal performance is more often than not a result of not feeling valued rather than a choice to underperform.

For many years, I worked in a highly unionized organization where labor contracts permitted union employees to work "at the minimal accepted level of productivity" with no risk of discipline. Such "slowdowns" were costly and often frustrating to managers. Equally as frustrating was the reason for such slowdowns. In most instances, it was because union members didn't feel listened to or valued for their opinions. Thus they resorted to costly and disruptive behavior to call attention to this fact. This is not unlike children who intentionally misbehave, knowing that even if they're attracting the wrong kind of attention, at least someone is noticing them.

I suggest that the 30-Day Process is a better way of addressing such issues. This is not to say you should do the process with a low performer *so that* he or she will improve. However, it's all but guaranteed that substantial improvements in performance and productivity will occur by the end of the process.

Choosing to do the process with a marginal performer is

a personal decision. It will vary from workplace to workplace and from individual to individual.

I have watched hundreds of people go through the 30-Day Process. Many were bosses with a number of direct reports; many were direct reports who did the process with their bosses. In every instance, where the intention was to motivate rather than to manipulate, success was virtually guaranteed. Even those who were skeptical in the beginning found themselves being won over by the willingness of another person to help them reconnect with their good qualities.

Once the question of intention and sincere motivation is resolved, the next challenge of the 30-Day Process is developing the determination to stay the course. That will be addressed in the next chapter.

CHAPTER SIX

PUTTING DOWN STAKES WHERE IT MATTERS

Habit is habit, and not to be flung out of the window by any man, but coaxed down stairs a step at a time.
—Mark Twain

For many of us, developing a new habit, such as the habit of acknowledgment, means letting go of other habits. The old way of doing things is a powerful opponent of even our best intentions. In many workshops, I have done an exercise in which I ask the participants to fold their arms across their chest. Then I ask them to do this again, only this time to reverse the position of their arms: in other words, if the left arm was on top before, to put the right arm on top and vice versa. There is usually some confusion and lots of laughter as people struggle to replace their old way of doing it with a new way.

Taking on the 30-Day Process can produce a similar kind of discomfort. When this happens, our flight instinct can take over and we start to look for "justifiable" reasons to abandon our commitment: an already busy work schedule, an active lifestyle, the fact that we've gotten along reasonably well without an affirming mind-set so far, all argue persuasively for postponing such an effort until "later."

When this kind of reasoning results in a breakdown of our resolve, I am reminded of some of the best advice I ever received. It was offered when I had tried twice—and failed twice—to successfully implement a customer service initiative in a department I was supervising. My instinct each time I failed was to look for something or someone to blame—or just to abandon the effort altogether. While that kind of thinking provided some relief in the short term, it did little to further my objective.

Following the second failure, a colleague stepped in and asked me why I wanted the customer service program in the first place. "What's at stake for you in getting this program up and running?" As I started to list the benefits to the staff, our company, and our customers, I realized that what my colleague had done was to reconnect me with my passion to provide extraordinary service. Passion creates possibilities. She followed up her comments with "When a breakdown occurs, focus on your intention, not the outcome."

The advice was simple enough, but the results were a different story. When the customer service program was finally up and running, it was so successful that other companies started to take notice. I eventually left the organization to set up a highly successful consulting practice that worked with businesses that wanted similar results with their own customer service initiatives.

Had my colleague's sage advice not come along when it did, I would probably still be looking for people to point the finger at, feeling justified in believing that my good ideas would never be implemented.

Because of what's at stake when businesses and individuals take on the task of intentional, sustaining acknowledgment, I thought it would be helpful to share what happened when others pushed through their own challenges in order to reap the benefits. These stories are taken from participants who completed the 30-Day Process.

THE VICE PRESIDENT AND THE SECRETARY

A senior vice president with a large health care organization who decided to do the 30-Day Process with her secretary admitted that halfway through the process she thought about giving up and regretted not having promised a smaller number of traits. However, she completed the process and said that once she got beyond her belief that she had run out of qualities, more and more things kept showing up for her to acknowledge.

On the feedback form, her secretary wrote, "I had no idea that [she] saw these qualities in me. It made me want to work all the harder for her. I also wanted to better develop some of the traits she shared with me. Even though we had a good relationship before the process started, what happened for us afterwards was amazing."

Not surprisingly, the vice president commented in her survey that her secretary's performance and productivity "shot through the roof. I had a hard time keeping her because all of the other vice presidents wanted her for their secretary." The secretary's loyalty, though, remained with the boss who had acknowledged her.

THE ASSISTANT AND THE DIRECTOR

An administrative assistant to one of the directors of a large manufacturing company wanted to do the 30-Day Process with her boss. In spite of the high trust they shared in their working relationship, she worried that he would think she was "bucking for a raise" by offering to share thirty traits over thirty days. However, she approached her boss with the idea, and he said he was flattered and honored that she wanted to take the time to do it.

About halfway through the process, she, too, "hit the wall" of believing that she had used up the supply of qualities she admired in her boss and wondered where the remaining traits would come from. "I started following my boss around, not literally, but with my eyes and ears. I watched him interact with other employees, with our vendors and suppliers, and realized how good he was at listening to their concerns. I heard him talking on the phone with a particularly difficult person without losing his cool.

"All at once I realized that the qualities of patience, tolerance, compassion, listening, and flexibility were all critical to his success, although I had never especially paid attention to them in that way."

She concluded by saying that once she had begun to appreciate these qualities, she had become eager to find more—and she did. By the end of the 30-Day Process she had a newfound appreciation for who this man was.

And so did he. His comments: "She put me in touch with aspects of myself that I hadn't thought about in a long time. It made me want to be a better boss and a better person. It's funny how taking the time to focus on what's working can shift one's perspective on lots of things."

TEAM SPIRIT

A work team of ten people in a large telecommunications company decided to do the 30-Day Process together as a way of deepening their respect for and connection with one another. They sat around a table at a Tuesday-morning staff meeting (where I, too, was present) and picked partners among themselves. Their approach was a bit unique in that each of them would be simultaneously on the giving *and* receiving end of the process, but with different partners. In other words, one of their teammates would be doing the process with them while they were doing the process with a different teammate at the same time.

Although this requires more of the participants, this particular team seemed to be up to the task. Six weeks later, I received feedback from 100 percent of the participants, all of whom had completed the process. They spoke about a renewed enthusiasm for their organization, their team, and themselves.

Apparently the organization took notice. The following year, when the company was cited for "extraordinary customer service" by one of its vendors at a national conference, a reporter asked the company president if his initiative had resulted in the award. Here was his response: "I can't take credit for this one. We had a team of people (guess which one?) in one of our divisions who seemed to outperform everyone when it came to customer service. So we started watching what they did and copied it. It was the damnedest thing. They seemed to really *like* themselves and our cus- tomers, saw things in them that we hadn't seen. So we decided to follow suit."

Note: Not all work teams are ideal candidates for the 30-Day Process. If you decide to initiate the process with your team, *all of the members* must be willing to participate, and they should already have a healthy respect for their fellow team members.

THE CEO AND THE CFO

The CEO of a small financial management company in the Midwest was a visionary in the truest sense of that word. His ability to envision an inspiring and profitable future for his small company resulted in employees who were as enthusiastic as they were competent.

Except one.

The CFO, who had been with the organization for almost six years, was brilliant as a number cruncher and was credited with meeting or exceeding earnings expectations most of that time. His ability to relate to others, however, was not as impressive. Staffers thought him unapproachable and inflexible when it came to tolerating new ideas.

The CEO asked the CFO if he could share thirty things he liked about him over the next thirty days. The CFO was not amused, seeing such an effort as a distraction from the more important task of fiscal responsibility. Since it was his boss who was making the request, however, he reluctantly agreed and resigned himself to what was about to happen.

At the end of the 30-Day Process, here's what each of them had to say:

The CEO: "Even though I knew he was a good man with a big heart, I had no idea just how good he was. When we began the process, his demeanor was so resistant that I wondered if I had made a mistake. I watched him soften as the days went by. I saw him relax into the process and start to actually ponder the truth of what I was sharing. I saw him take ownership of all of who he is, not just the part that does his job well."

The CFO: "As far as I was concerned, this process was something to be endured. The first few days [the CEO] didn't tell me anything I didn't already know about myself. One day, though, he told me he admired my tolerance for new ideas. How did he know that? I had come to believe that tolerating the ideas of others meant that my own competence was somehow lacking, even though some of the ideas I heard from others were worth considering. It was as if he saw through me to what was really inside. I felt freed up to let this side of me show up."

The employees noticed the changes as well. At the company's next annual awards luncheon, the CFO received the "favorite staffer" award.

These stories are offered as a reminder that our willingness to stay the course when it comes to acknowledging others can have significant payoffs, for individuals as well as the organization.

When you experience your own resistance to keeping a thirty-day promise because it seems too difficult or too time-consuming, ask yourself if increased productivity, high morale, reduced turnover, and a passion for the job are sufficient stakes for staying the course.

In the next two chapters, we'll talk about the residuals that come with successfully completing the 30-Day Process —its self-affirming nature and its domino effect.

CHAPTER SEVEN

IT TAKES ONE TO KNOW ONE

I RESEMBLE THAT REMARK.

—CURLY HOWARD

When people first hear about the 30-Day Process, many of them get very excited . . . about being on the *receiving* end. While we may concede the value and benefit of acknowledging another person, inwardly what we really want is to be acknowledged ourselves. After all, wouldn't this be the perfect opportunity to reconnect with what we've suspected all along, that we are uniquely praiseworthy and innately good? Even a person who jokes about the improbability of someone finding thirty things in him or her to appreciate secretly hopes (and knows, I believe) that it can be done. This desire to be acknowledged for who we are confirms that our greatest psychological need as human beings is to be validated, to know that we matter. Giving someone else something we want so much for ourselves may seem like a delaying tactic for our own unmet needs.

When I did the 30-Day Process with Kelly in 1996, I was neither seeking for nor expecting it to be self-affirming. This was to be about Kelly and what I admired about her. What I had forgotten, but nonetheless already believed, is that what we give away comes back to us. And this is exactly what happens with the 30-Day Process. Some of the exhilaration I felt at the end of our process related to how I now perceived myself. Helping Kelly connect with her own goodness automatically connected me with my own.

This so-called mirroring effect is not new. Dr. Cheri Carter-Scott in her book *If Life Is a Game, These Are the Rules* states in Rule 7, "Others are only mirrors of you." Or consider the Hindu proverb that says, "Help thy brother's boat across and lo! Thine own has reached the shore." And an Asian saying reminds us that "He makes things easier for himself who makes things easier for others."

The flip side of this mirroring effect is also true. The great singer Marian Anderson said, "As long as you keep a person down, some part of you has to be down there to hold him down, so it means you cannot soar as you otherwise might."

Maria Nemeth, writing in her book *The Energy of Money,* asks readers to define qualities that they admire in others as part of a process of determining an individual's standards for integrity. Once the list of qualities has been identified, she says, "Take the new list and place it in front of you. Each trait has significance and meaning for you. That is because you possess the receptor site for it in your heart. If you didn't know what each quality meant, it would not have the power to evoke a response from you. To put this another way: if you see these qualities in others, then they exist in you. If not, you would not be able to see them in others."

She concludes by saying, "You possess the qualities you see in others. You possess the qualities you listed. They are part of your nature. You can't get rid of them no matter what you do."

My first experience with this mirroring concept came when I was a participant in a training class many years ago. One of the exercises we were asked to do divided us into groups of six or eight. We were instructed to tell each of the others in the group one thing we appreciated about him or her. This in itself didn't seem so hard until we were instructed to begin our sharing by saying, "What I see in you *that I like about myself* is . . ." and then complete the sentence with an admired quality or trait. This was unsettling. It was one thing to say something nice about the others in the group, but having to confess that I saw those same qualities in myself was unnerving. Wouldn't that sound boastful? Wouldn't it diminish the value of what I saw in others?

Since I am usually one to err on the side of "looking good," I boldly offered to go first. The first time or two I shared, using the required preface, I felt some embarrassment. Then I started to relax and get into the swing of it. By the time I had completed the circle, it was no big deal. When I asked the facilitator why putting the "myself" phrase in there was a required part of the exercise, he simply responded, "Because it's true."

The trainers' theory, in which I now heartily concur, is that we are incapable of seeing in others that which does not already exist in ourselves. For example, when I acknowledge someone at work for his or her professional demeanor, it must be a value that already exists in me or I probably would not have noticed it in them. My idea of professional demeanor may be quite different from theirs, but the value is nonetheless one that is shared. Likewise, if I praise a coworker for attendance and punctuality, it's because that's something I value, too. If I acknowledge my boss for having a great sense of humor, it's because I value that quality in myself as well. And so on.

As the feedback from 30-Day Process participants has repeatedly shown, one of its most pleasant surprises comes when we realize that what we are doing when we acknowledge another person is shining a spotlight on our own qualities.

Let's consider what happens when this occurs.

In the early days of my research on the impact of sustained, intentional acknowledgment, I asked many friends, family members, and work colleagues to try the 30-Day Process and give me their feedback. Many who did suggested that I write a book about the process. In the beginning, this was an easy suggestion to discount, since writing was not a part of my history, experience, or competence, so far as I knew. After all, I was someone who earned her living as a speaker, not a writer.

It was at about this same time that I elected to do the 30-Day Process with my husband, Tom. One of the things I acknowledged him for was being "clever with words." (The next chapter tells what he did when I mentioned this trait.) When I began to understand the mirroring aspect of affirming someone else, this particular trait struck a chord with *me*, since it seemed to negate my belief that I was not a writer.

A funny thing happens when you connect with an aspect of yourself that has long been hidden or denied: it begs to be revealed, to be used. Very slowly but very surely, the idea of writing a book about acknowledgment began to seem less and less absurd to me.

If you're still reading at this point, you know how this story ends.

One of my former work colleagues, who elected to do the 30-Day Process with one of her children, realized that more than anything else she loved the impact that her daughter's playfulness had on others. The quality of "playfulness" apparently touched off something in herself, because all of a sudden we had a playful colleague at work whose lightness unleashed some of our most creative ideas.

There is an interesting, if unfortunate, irony in this mirroring. Many of us are quick to see qualities in others that we absolutely deny could exist in ourselves. This is based less on truth than it is on our human nature to believe that while others may have their worthy-of-praise act together, we ourselves are still very much a work in progress.

This became apparent when I was talking with a former client in the oil services industry. He was quite willing to see the goodness in others but had a hard time believing that any of if existed in him. I suggested he do the 30-Day Process with himself, focusing each day for thirty days on a different quality that he admired about himself. He laughed as if I had just asked the impossible. I then asked him if he could find thirty things that annoyed him about himself. His good-natured response: "I can have that list over to you in thirty minutes!"

This validates my belief that we have no problem with focusing on our own shortcomings, but we are slow to acknowledge our good qualities.

This was brought home to me in a very real way a number of years ago when I was still living in Arlington, Virginia. My friend Joyce Shuman and I played singles tennis on a weekly basis. One morning as we were playing, we observed that while each of us was quick to praise the playing efforts of the other, we were singularly critical of our own performance. While I may have occasionally made a great drop shot, what I actually commented about was a poor second serve or an unforced error. Further, when Joyce or I told each other good things about our play, we each tended to discount what the other said. For example, if Joyce said to me, "Great second serve, Dottie!," I would respond with something to the effect of "Yeah, but what about that lousy first one?"

As is often the case when someone else praises us or offers us a compliment, our training and tendency are to discount the remark or at best become deferential. The way I played tennis, in other words, was not unlike the way I played my life, offering up the appropriate version of "This old dress? I've had it forever" when someone offered me a compliment.

When I shared this observation with Joyce, we decided to change the "verbal" rules of how we played tennis: We would not comment on the good play of our partner until and unless we had first commented on our own good play. Also, we would not verbally acknowledge any poor efforts; we would just be silent about what we were *not* doing well and focus instead on what we *were* doing well. We were creating our own version of "If you can't say anything nice, don't say anything at all."

What started out as a lighthearted experiment quickly

became more serious when we played our next three games in silence. We had such an ingrained habit of self-criticism that it was difficult to notice ourselves doing anything right, never mind have the presence of mind to comment on it. In other words, it was easier to play in silence than it was to focus on what we were doing right—and comment on it. Finally, we started—somewhat shyly at first—to praise ourselves for good shots. When we intentionally paid attention to what was working and verbally patted ourselves on the back for it, we started to realize that both of us really played tennis very well.

My assessment of my tennis game shifted from all of the errors I needed to work on to how well I played many of my shots. I began to expect myself to play good tennis—and I did.

A footnote to this story: While neither Joyce nor I wound up on the pro circuit, I had occasion to be reminded of our experiment during the televised coverage of Wimbledon in 1999, when I watched Steffi Graf play in the women's singles final. When the television cameras panned over to Steffi's mom sitting in the stands, one commentator asked the other if she knew whether or not Mrs. Graf had been the typical "stage mom," pushing her daughter to extremes to succeed. The response was a refreshing "no." The second commentator went on to say that when Steffi had lost a match as a young player, her mother had always hugged her, praised her play that day, and told her she was confident she would play better the next time.

As the next story demonstrates, while it's great to have someone else there to cheer us on, we don't always need a partner to help us make this shift in perception.

A friend of mine who graduated from ministerial school wanted to try the 30-Day Process. His somewhat solitary lifestyle and admitted lack of self-esteem caused him to conclude that he probably wouldn't be successful with the process. As with my oil industry friend, I suggested he do the process with himself; that once a day, over the next thirty days, he identify qualities he admired and appreciated about himself. He did. Here's what happened, in his words:

> *I finally figured out that I'm a good guy! My confirming for myself what others have told me for years was uplifting. Living alone does not always give me the positive strokes I want from others. The process meant me taking time for me. I tend to put myself last, so the 30-Day Process gave me time to remind myself of my goodness.*
>
> *I kept a journal by my bed and wrote my qualities in it each night. By the time I completed the process, I could see a huge difference in my self-esteem and self-worth. What a gift!*

Another interesting aspect of mirroring is that it can awaken qualities that may have been dormant for a while and are now rekindled. While I have always considered myself to be a mother whose heart was in the right place, where the role of coach was concerned, I had taken a rather sharp detour. It took the coaching of my daughter Rebecca to reconnect me with that quality.

During Rebecca's teen years, her desire for adventure far exceeded my comfort level. In fact, I used to quip to my friends that I was confident Rebecca would survive her teen years, but I wasn't so sure her mother would. When Rebecca was seventeen, I decided to pull out all the stops and make one last effort to get her to see life the "right" way, that is, from my perspective. I found a week-long self-improvement course in the mountains of California and told Rebecca that I thought our attending it together would be a great "bonding" experience. Secretly I was hoping that Rebecca would attend, see the error of her ways, and return with profound gratitude for a mother who cared so much about her.

Since Rebecca was not one to turn down a free trip to California, we headed off.

On our first day in class, the facilitator asked Rebecca how she would characterize her teen years. She answered, "I've been grounded most of them!" This was hardly the response I had hoped for, since it implied that her parents were little more than benevolent jailers. That night in our room, I chastised Rebecca gently and suggested she might want to be more careful in choosing her responses.

The week progressed and lots of changes occurred. But nothing could have prepared me for what happened on our last day in the course. When the facilitator asked if anyone had any closing observations, Rebecca's hand shot up. I shuddered at what might be coming. Here's what she said:

> When I showed up here on Monday, I thought of my parents mostly as enforcers of punishment and myself as the one on whom the punishment was enforced. What I realize now is that they are really coaches who want the best for me. Grounding me when

*I violate one of the rules is just their way of coaching
me. So I want to acknowledge my mom for being my
coach.*

It was Rebecca's ability to "coach" her mother that
reminded me of a role too long buried.

This incident happened almost fourteen years ago, and it
was a turning point in our relationship—and in my life.
Rebecca saw in me something I had long since buried
beneath my determination to have her walk the straight and
narrow. I did, in fact, consider part of my role as a mother to
be that of a coach. But the idea had gotten lost somewhere
along the way. Rebecca saw it and revealed it, and nothing
has been the same between us since. It became so much
more fun to be her coach than her jailer. My behavior
changed, and so did hers.

My point in sharing this story is that celebrating what
you see in others, even when they can't see it clearly for
themselves, not only has a mirroring effect but also is a way
of putting us in touch with those parts of ourselves that
somehow have become relegated to the back burner.

A manager who did the 30-Day Process with one of his
direct reports said that focusing on her good qualities had
made him more conscious of wanting to develop those same
qualities in himself: "When I think about how great it is to
have someone in the workplace who possesses so many great
qualities, it makes me want others to see those qualities in
me as well."

For those of you who doubt that your own good qualities will be revealed in sharing with another, I urge you to try

the 30-Day Process and see for yourself. Sharing others' good qualities with them really does reveal our own.

In addition to mirroring, there is another residual benefit that comes from doing the process, and that is the domino or ripple effect. Let's take a closer look at this impact.

CHAPTER EIGHT

THE ACKNOWLEDGMENT DOMINO EFFECT

WHEN SOMEONE DOES SOMETHING NICE FOR ME, I TURN AROUND AND DO SOMETHING NICE FOR SOMEONE ELSE. THAT'S THE DOMINO EFFECT AT ITS BEST!
   —LOUISE HAY, *YOU CAN HEAL YOUR LIFE*

Perhaps one of the most rewarding benefits of the act of acknowledgment is the domino effect it seems to have. In other words, putting in a kind word here and there, doing a good deed, and using the 30-Day Process to express appreciation to those most important to you all have residual benefits. Earlier this year I was a participant in a class in which one of my colleagues said that the production of residual income is one of his financial goals. He went on to say that he wants to make the kind of investments now that will continue to have payoffs in the future. The same can be said for practicing acknowledgment: action taken today will continue to have benefits in the future.

Over and over again, organizations have discovered that taking great care of their employees is also a great way to take care of business. In other words, what starts at the top has a beneficial trickle-down effect on the bottom line.

I recall going into Schlotzky's Deli in the town of Allen, Texas, where I live, and being greeted effusively by the young man who took my order. He seemed to be in a great mood and wanted to go out of his way to provide excellent service. When I commented on his enthusiasm, he responded by telling me that he had just come from a managers' meeting where his boss had publicly praised him for doing a great job. He went on to say that this had made him feel so good that "nothing could keep me down today!" In other words, what had happened in that managers' meeting only a few hours earlier was having a domino effect on this young man's performance.

I have told this story many times since, saying that anyone who wants good service should visit Schlotzky's Deli in Allen, Texas.

I have also wondered what the service would have been like that day if he had been chewed out by his boss instead of praised.

Fortunately, more and more businesses have caught on to the notion that when their employees feel valued, the benefits are manifold. Consider Blair Corporation and the domino impact of a single piece of promotional literature.

Once while I was conducting a corporate workshop based on the 30-Day Process, one of the participants pulled out a promotional letter she had received with some catalog items she had ordered from Blair Corporation. Blair was founded in 1910 in Warren, Pennsylvania, and sells fashion apparel for men and women as well as home products, primarily by mail. As a way of acknowledging its customers and employees, Blair includes a letter with each shipment. This letter has photographs of some of the employees who were personally involved in the production, order entry, and shipment of the products. Each person has signed his or her name below his or her photograph. Part of the letter says, "We speak for over 2200 fellow employees who genuinely appreciate your business. . . . THANK YOU!" The letter goes on to talk about Blair's money-back guarantee and other information related to the customer's purchase.

The participant in my class who shared this story said she had been so impressed by this "personal" acknowledgment of her purchase that she wanted to share the letter, a copy of which she was carrying in her organizer, with us. I asked for a photocopy of the letter, as did others. In subsequent workshops I have shown this letter as an example of how customers are acknowledged when employees are acknowledged. Each time I show the letter, I am asked for copies, which I give out freely. I don't know how many customers this is creating for Blair, but the domino effect seems to keep on going.

Consider also what a Dallas-based insurance group did. In an effort to encourage behavior that demonstrated its core values, Hallmark Financial decided to link an acknowledgment activity with those values. Cards were made that highlighted the company values of teamwork, integrity, and excellence. Spaces were provided for the name of the giver as well as the recipient, along with the date and a brief explanation.

The cards were given to the officers, supervisors, and team leaders of the company, who in turn were asked to hand them out *on the spot* to team members seen exhibiting behaviors reflective of the company's core values. The recipients of these cards would be announced at the monthly breakfast meeting attended by the company's 140 employees. In addition to this monthly recognition, recipients are also eligible for drawings for other prizes.

Linda Sleeper, a good friend of mine and the company's CEO, elected to take the acknowledgment part of this activity to another level. She decided to honor the company's CFO, who had been the initial catalyst for the acknowledgment cards. What she did was revealed at the next monthly breakfast meeting.

Linda wrote a poem in which she acknowledged the attributes of the CFO and enlisted the rest of the company to join in with her on the last line when she read the poem to him at the meeting. The reading of the poem turned out to be a huge success, especially when everyone joined in on the poem's last line, which said, in part, "and we all really like you." So touched was the CFO by what had happened that he asked Linda if he could have a copy of the poem to take home to read to his wife. Linda complied with his request, and the poem and employee went home for the weekend.

On Monday morning, Linda asked the CFO if he had indeed read the poem to his wife. He said that he had. When asked how she had responded, he said her reply had been "I didn't know that's how they felt." The CFO then told Linda that he hadn't known, either, how his colleagues felt about him, even though he had worked with many of them for nine years.

As it turns out, there was an interesting ripple effect from all of this initiative at Hallmark Financial. I was so impressed with what Linda and her colleagues had done that I decided that I could write a poem, too. Linda and I both serve on the board of directors of the Unity Church of Dallas. Linda, in fact, was the president of the board at the time I learned what Hallmark was doing. When her term was up in April 2000, the board wanted to find a way to express its appreciation to Linda for her tireless services. Our decision? You guessed it: I agreed to write a poem similar to the one Linda had written for her CFO, and the entire board joined in on the last line, which, of course, included "and we really like you!"

There is a postscript to this story: Impressed with the impact that acknowledgment was having in the workplace, Linda decided to have personal acknowledgment cards made up. She intends to hand these out to people who provide good service, offer help, express a kind word, and so on. We can only speculate on what will happen to those who receive Linda's cards and what they might decide to do in turn.

Remember in the previous chapter when I said there was more to add about when I told my husband that he was clever with words? Here's the domino impact of that trait, as expressed in Tom's own words:

I was convinced that nothing about this process would "change" me. In fact, I was probably on guard against being "fixed" or unduly influenced toward a direction I might not want to go. What did happen was totally unexpected and I am convinced would never have happened without this process.

One of the things Dottie acknowledged me for was

being clever. The example she used was that I was "clever with words." This acknowledgment gave me the inspiration to begin to write poetry. What I discovered was that I had a flair and a talent for doing this. I eventually wrote a whole volume of poetry with a special emphasis on sonnets. Out of that writing experience came an idea for a gift item for which I have now received a U.S. patent.

I know that I would never have had the courage to write poetry without the acknowledgment. And without the poetry, I would never have thought of the gift line. I don't know where all of this will eventually end up, but I have discovered aspects of my abilities that would have remained hidden even from myself without the acknowledgment process.

A follow-up to this story concerns a presentation that Tom and I made on the subject of relationships. Tom decided to include some of his poetry as a demonstration of one of the points we were making. The response was overwhelming, so much so that our presentation has now been turned into a workshop, which, of course, will feature Tom's poetry for sale at the back of the room.

Another good example of the domino effect of acknowledgment came from a friend of mine. I'll let Nancy Connors tell you that story herself:

Twenty years ago, I had an experience that changed the way I look at people in my everyday life. I was a classroom teacher with a master's degree, and I was accustomed to being treated as a professional. Yet when a friend with a catering business was desperate for some extra help in catering a large wedding, I volunteered to help out.

Decked out in a white blouse and black skirt, I carried trays of hors d'oeuvres and refilled champagne glasses. As I waited on the wealthy crowd by emptying ashtrays and serving meals, it soon became apparent that in my new service position people treated me very differently. No longer was I a respected professional; it seemed that donning the uniform of hired help had made me invisible. This startling revelation made me rethink the way I treated others around me. As I thought about the many service people I encountered in a typical week, I realized that I, too, often treated those people as invisible. I vowed to change.

A year or so later, I was on a business trip in a large city. I had gotten up at first light to go on a brisk morning walk. I cut through a wide alley as I headed back to the hotel and came face-to-face with a man in a dark jumpsuit working on early-morning garbage collection. As he hoisted an overflowing trash can onto his shoulder, I nodded at him and said, "Beautiful day, isn't it?" "It is now," he responded with a shy grin.

With the knowledge that all people in every station of life have a basic need for validation, my husband and I have made it a practice to make eye contact with all those we encounter. At the movie theater we frequent, a severely handicapped young man takes the tickets. His crippled and floundering hands as well as his low posi-

tion in a wheelchair make it somewhat awkward for the patrons, and we have observed that everyone seems to thrust their tickets in his face and rush past him without so much as a glance in his direction.

We make it a point to stop and say hello and ask how his day is going. The change in his demeanor has been tremendous on those occasions. We have seen his bowed head look up with a crooked grin and beaming face. After the first such encounter, he remembered us and now makes a point to personally welcome us when we attend that theater.

Acknowledgment. It is such a simple act and yet one that often remains undone.

One of my favorite stories about this effect was shared with me by a colleague who is a schoolteacher.

She told me about a teacher in New York City who decided to honor each of her seniors in high school by telling them the difference each of them had made in her life. She called each student to the front of the class, one at a time. First, she told each student how he or she had made a difference to her and the class. Then she presented him or her with a blue ribbon imprinted in gold with "Who I am makes a difference."

Afterward the teacher decided to do a class project to see what kind of impact recognition would have on a community. She gave the students three more ribbons each and instructed them to go out and repeat this acknowledgment ceremony. Then they were to follow up on the results, see who they honored, and report back to the class in about a week.

One of the boys in the class went to a junior executive in

a nearby company and honored him for helping him with his career planning. He gave him one of the blue ribbons and put it on his shirt. Then he gave him his two other ribbons and said, "We're doing a class project on recognition, and we'd like you to go out, find somebody to honor, and give them a blue ribbon. Then give them the extra blue ribbon so they can acknowledge a third person to keep this acknowledgment ceremony going. Then please report back and tell me what happened."

Later that day the junior executive went in to see his boss, who had a reputation as something of a grouch. He sat his boss down and told him that he deeply admired him for being a creative genius. The boss seemed very surprised. The junior executive asked him if he would accept the gift of a blue ribbon and if he would give him permission to put it on him.

His surprised boss concurred and proudly displayed the ribbon on his jacket. The junior executive gave him the last ribbon and asked him to pass it on by honoring someone else. He explained that the young boy who had given him his ribbon was involved in a recognition project. The boss agreed to pass along the last ribbon.

That night the boss went home to his fourteen-year-old son and sat him down. He said, "The most incredible thing happened to me today. I was in my office, and one of the junior executives came in and told me he admired me and gave me a blue ribbon for being a creative genius. Imagine, he thinks I'm a creative genius! Then he pinned this blue ribbon that says 'Who I am makes a difference' on my jacket above my heart. He gave me an extra ribbon and asked me to find somebody else to honor.

"As I was driving home tonight, I started thinking about

who I would honor with this ribbon, and I thought about you. I want to honor you. My days are really hectic, and when I come home I don't always pay a lot of attention to you. Sometimes I yell at you for not getting good enough grades in school and for your bedroom being a mess, but tonight I just wanted to sit here and, well, just let you know that you do make a difference to me. Besides your mother, you are the most important person in my life. You're a great kid, and I love you."

His son was taken aback and began to cry. He looked at his father and confessed that he had come to believe that he was an unimportant and forgotten part of his father's life . . . but not anymore.

I would like to close this chapter with a personal story about what happened when I decided to try a random process of acknowledgment. I was listening to an audiotape lecture in which the lecturer said that one of the ways she kept herself centered was to silently "bless" everyone around her, whether they were driving in front of her on the freeway, standing behind her in the checkout line, or performing their duties at work. Thinking this would be a good way to pass the time on the indoor jogging track at the gym, I decided to silently "bless" everyone I saw. Here's what happened.

The track is on the second level of the gym and is open to the floor below, where you can observe people working out on exercise machines, swimming laps in the pool, or lifting weights. I decided to look at all these people and just silently say, "Bless you." I was happily engaged in this activity when I noticed a man walking on the track about thirty yards in front of me. Thinking he would be my next candidate to "bless," I hesitated as I got close enough to see his long hair, his heavily tattooed arms, and what appeared to be a Harley-Davidson emblem on the back of his shirt. I noticed my hesitancy and felt somewhat sheepish that I found myself now wanting to engage in a selection process for who got "blessed." As I caught up with him on the track, I noticed that his shirt said something about a Vietnam veterans' reunion in South Carolina. I thought about this, and the next time I passed him on the track, I asked him if he himself was a Vietnam vet. He said that he was, and we both kept on with our walking and jogging. I found myself becoming curious about him, so on the next pass, I asked his name and he said quietly, "Greg."

Every morning after that, I saw Greg working out with weights or on the track. One morning I stopped him and asked him if he would tell me about himself. He told me that he was indeed a Vietnam vet and that he remained active in causes important to those very special veterans. He told me he had been in the corporate world for many years and that he and his wife had recently decided to opt for a simpler lifestyle. He told me they had sold their large home and were now living comfortably in smaller quarters.

He said that he had had an injury that had gotten him started coming to the gym for rehab, and that he had chosen to continue coming to help stay fit. He talked about his efforts on behalf of Vietnam veterans and how little people seemed to care about what had happened to them anymore. He shared all of this without bitterness or remorse, just a gentle man quietly telling his story.

I share my encounter with him because it is a conversation that would never have occurred had I not been willing to indiscriminately and without exception acknowledge everyone I saw at the gym that particular day.

This encounter happened in 1999, and I haven't seen Greg in a while. Perhaps he's moved on, but I am so grateful he found his way across my path that day.

I am also grateful for people like Hilary Johnson, the front-desk person at that same gym (Bally's in Plano, Texas), who shows up every morning at 5:00 A.M. so that people like myself can have a place to work out at our convenience. Unlike many of us at that hour, Hilary is friendly and cheerful. In fact, she's one of the reasons I manage to get there every day—if Hilary can get up early every morning, so can I!

People like her do the jobs and work the hours that make it possible for each of us to enjoy a more workable lifestyle. They are deserving of our appreciation and expressed acknowledgment. They are like silent partners in helping make our lives work.

That's what acknowledgment does—it removes the barriers to our understanding what is true and good about others.

CHAPTER NINE

EVEN MORE WAYS TO CELEBRATE YOU

DOES A HERO KNOW SHE'S A HERO IF NO ONE TELLS HER?
—NIKE MAGAZINE AD

The purpose of the 30-Day Process is to develop the *habit of acknowledgment.* It is a creative and useful tool for sharpening our commitment to letting those around us know how much we care about them and depend on them. As with any such commitment, once the skill is in place, it's time to maintain it through ongoing activities that ensure that what we know and what we do are aligned. Just as reading a diet book doesn't cause you to lose weight, neither does knowing the power of acknowledgment work without regular application. This chapter offers examples of what other individuals and organizations have done and are doing to celebrate the achievements of their work colleagues. I encourage you to follow suit.

MAKE ME A POSTER CHILD

The Coastal Alliance Group, based in Midland, Texas, was a consortium of oil field services companies that joined forces to bid on large projects. Since many of the participating companies were quite small, forming such an alliance seemed to be a reasonable solution. This group was led by my good friend Bruce Lowe.

As a consultant to the alliance, I traveled with alliance members to New Mexico to facilitate a working retreat in 1996. That the structure of the alliance had a deep bonding effect on its members was evidenced in the way they related to one another professionally. At this particular retreat, we decided to take these relationships to another level.

On the first day of our three-day meeting, we posted a blank flip chart page for each person present, with his or her name at the top of the page. These flip chart pages covered most of the wall space of our meeting room. We asked all those present, over the next three days, to write down one trait or quality that they admired or appreciated about each person on the appropriate flip chart sheet. On the last day of the retreat, each sheet contained about twenty qualities (one for each person who attended), and we left them posted for everyone to see. Then we had each participant take down his or her sheet and read the qualities aloud to the rest of the group. This turned out to be a defining moment as the alliance partners in the room reflected on the qualities and competencies of each person. This process is easy to replicate by any team or group.

I'M GOING TO TELL YOUR MOTHER WHAT YOU DID!

Writing in *Sam's Club Magazine,* Bob Nelson, a motivational speaker, told about a former supervisor at MCI who had energized a team of telemarketers working for him. "Our group was the worst-performing sales group at the time. I nicknamed it the 'F-Troop' and told my manager that I'd make them the best-performing group in three months. He thought I was crazy. On the spur of the moment one day, I told the group that if they got to be number one, I'd call their mothers and tell them how great they were."

As individuals met their performance goals, he did just that. He went on to say, "I couldn't have predicted the impact of doing this! Some moms cried, while others were excited. All were proud. I'm sure as soon as we hung up, they each immediately called their son or daughter to tell them they had just spoken to their boss and what was said. Each employee came to work the next day feeling and acting like a champion. We reached our goal of becoming number one in the company, and for many of the employees it was the start of new levels of performance and better things to come."

And here are more ideas.

'TIS THE SEASON TO BE JOLLY

A friend sent me an e-mail that told about a process used by another office group, this time during the holiday season. Becoming tired of the let's-draw-a-name-and-buy-a-gag-gift routine, someone suggested a different approach for the upcoming Christmas holiday: that they give one another the "gift" of acknowledgment. A few days before Christmas, the team of six people gathered in one of the offices and set up some ground rules for the acknowledgment process. The guidelines included things such as the person being acknowledged saying no more than "Thanks." Those who felt uncomfortable giving or receiving their acknowledgment in public could request to do so in private.

The e-mail I received went on to report that each team member started his or her communication by saying to each colleague, "[*name*], the gift you give me is . . ." As the process continued, the participants began to see qualities in others they hadn't noticed before. Their conclusion? The spirit and connectedness they shared in that process became larger than the group. They were "humbled and enriched" by what they had learned about one another. The cost? A willingness to see the gifts in others and to speak about them out loud.

MIXING PRAISE WITH PROFITS

Howard Ross, a former business partner in Washington, D.C., and I used a similar method during our weekly staff phone call. Since we were all working in various home offices, we conferenced by phone each Monday morning to set up our respective workweeks. As part of this call, we asked each person to be prepared to say one thing he or she admired about each of the others on the call. As soon as we got over the initial awkwardness of hearing our praises sung by our work colleagues, we looked forward to completing the weekly business aspect of the call so that we could get to the acknowledgment part. As a result we worked well as a team and were highly successful as a business.

WHEN BOASTING BECOMES ROASTING

Contrast these results with those of another organization that proposed a similar form of acknowledgment. In this organization, one of the regions began each Monday morning with a conference call that linked field representatives with the headquarters staff. The suggestion was made that each week an individual on the team would be randomly selected to be the surprise recipient of an acknowledgment. Another individual on the team would do the "homework" on this person and present the findings to the group on the weekly call. The person doing the acknowledging was to share the attributes without naming the recipient up front. The idea was to guess who best fit the positive profile being offered, and then everyone would "applaud and cheer" that person.

The process worked well for a couple of weeks. Then the person assigned to do the homework on the following week's surprise recipient decided to make a joke out of the assignment. During the next Monday-morning call, embarrassing incidents from the recipient's past were brought up and jokes were made about that person's appearance and personality. Some of those on the call were horrified. Regretfully, most of them thought it very clever, and for the next several weeks what had started out as a way of honoring team members degenerated into a "roast." Not surprisingly, the so-called acknowledgment process eventually faded away. No effort was made to put it back on its original track. Only three of the original eighteen members of this team remain in the organization.

But let's get back to more examples of successful ways businesses and individuals can go about affirming others.

WRITE ONE DOWN AND PASS IT AROUND

This example has its origin in a training class I attended in the mid-1980s. At one point in the training, we were seated in a large circle and asked to pull out a sheet of blank paper and put our name on the top. Each person then passed the sheet of paper to the left and the next person wrote down a quality or trait he or she admired or appreciated about the one whose name was at the top. This process went on until we all received our own sheet of paper back, filled, in this case, with forty-six qualities and traits offered by those in the class.

While some people are quick to suggest that such processes are little other than an attempt to embarrass those participating, these kinds of comments can also have a lasting positive impact.

TAKE A NOTE . . . LITERALLY

During an interview to promote the movie *The Hurricane*, Denzel Washington told of the time when he had been a twenty-year-old college dropout. He was in his mother's beauty shop one day when a woman wrote on a piece of paper, "This boy is going to speak to millions of people." In time that fateful meeting persuaded Mr. Washington to give college another try—and there he discovered his acting talent. Denzel Washington had no way of knowing at the time what the words on that piece of paper meant. But he treasured those words, and, as we all know, he went on to make a huge impact on the lives of millions—and continues to do so. Another thing: He still has that piece of paper that was handed to him so many years ago. "I keep it with me all the time," he says.

USING DAVID LETTERMAN'S "TOP 10" IDEA TO PRAISE

Pat Jonz and two other managers of Diagnostic Imaging at Presbyterian Hospital in Greenville, Texas, decided to use David Letterman's "Top 10" format as a way of acknowledging their staff during National Radiologic Technology Week. Because their staff of sixty was scattered over three shifts, seven days a week, Pat and her colleagues elected to use e-mail as their way of communicating with everyone. Monday through Friday of the week selected, Pat and her colleagues e-mailed "two things we love about you" each day to the staff. They were praised for going the extra mile, being loyal, being great problem solvers, exhibiting professionalism, taking pride in themselves and the job they did, and so on.

When I asked Pat where her desire to be so affirming had come from, she responded, "My boss is a master of acknowledging, and it feels so good we wanted to pass it on." This kind of affirming culture seems to have payoffs for this group in that the turnover rate among the technical staff is very low. A radiologic technologist who lives in Shreveport, Louisiana, during the week commutes to the hospital to work shifts totaling forty hours every weekend. And he tells everyone how proud he is of his job.

YOU'RE MY PERSON OF THE YEAR!

A good friend and former work colleague, Pam Walsh, lives in Orem, Utah, where she operates Courage, Inc., a highly successful national coaching practice. In one year-end issue of her *Courage Report* newsletter, she asked, "Are there a select few people in your life who have impacted you this year in ways that are priceless to you? If your answer is yes, how about letting them know it in a special way, by naming them one of your very own *People of the Year*?"

Pam went on to offer guidelines for making these people feel very special. She suggested jotting down specifically what the person had done that had impacted us so much. We were urged to think of an actual story that described the contribution of the person as well. "The better you describe what the person did, and the more the person understands the value he/she has added," Pam noted, "the greater the compliment you give them."

Being intrigued with this idea, I asked Pam to have any of her clients who would be willing to share the outcome of such a process contact me.

One of the people I interviewed, from Reston, Virginia, said that he had been doing the "Person of the Year" process since 1993. Each year he picks one or two people and sends them a plaque framed to resemble the *Time* magazine "Man/Woman of the Year" issue. The cover has a picture of the recipient with a subheadline that describes that person's unique contribution to his life. His recipients have included a boss, a coworker, a neighbor, a friend, and, in 1999, someone whom he had never met, New York mayor Rudolph Giuliani.

He described returning to New York City after a twenty-year absence and finding himself in awe of its beauty and buildings and natural landscapes. A city he had once regarded as dirty and unfriendly had been "transformed by the vision and by the courage of a man who loves the city and wanted to see it look and function as it should." In an age when it is fashionable to criticize politicians, this man chose to salute "a man I have never met as my person of the year for 1999."

Another person I interviewed was from Boulder, Colorado. She described how she had identified her three "People of the Year." She told of sending e-mails to the two principals of her children's respective schools. She described one of the principals as "someone who stuck with me and helped me figure things out." The other principal provided "direction and follow-through when I needed it most." Both of these persons had helped her as a parent in a way that made a difference, so she had named them both "Person of the Year." The third person she selected was the senior minister at her church, whom she had watched handle several church crises "with grace." She wanted him to know that his behavior and actions had been appreciated by her.

Variations of this process could be used very successfully in business environments as a way of honoring team members, either on a formalized basis throughout the organization or by team leaders wanting to make acknowledgment a priority in their group.

THE "FRUITS" OF OUR LABORS

Finally, I want to share one of my favorite stories about the role that spontaneity can play in creating a workplace acknowledgment process. My friend Eric Harvey, who owns the Walk the Talk Company in Dallas, recently published a booklet called "180 Ways to Walk the Recognition Talk," in which he tells a story about the Foxboro Company. It seems that in its early days the company was desperately in need of a technological advance in order to stay in business.

Late one evening a scientist rushed into the president's office with a working prototype. It was just what the company needed to stay afloat.

Dumbfounded by the elegance of the solution and wanting to reward his colleague on the spot, the president bent forward in his chair, rummaged through his desk drawers, found something, leaned over the desk toward the scientist, and said, "Here!"

In his hand was a banana—the only reward he could immediately put his hands on.

From that point on, a small "gold banana" pin has been the highest accolade for scientific achievement at Foxboro.

These ideas are but a few examples of what creative minds and great intentions can produce. I urge you to do the same. If you are uncertain what might work with your particular team or staff, there's one surefire way of finding out: ask! I think you'll be surprised and pleased by what you hear. After all, surveys tell us that a simple, timely thank-you, spoken or offered in a written note, can have a significant impact.

Whatever your decision, now would be a good time to start.

CHAPTER TEN

(AP)PRAISING PERFORMANCE

I LONG TO ACCOMPLISH A GREAT AND NOBLE TASK, BUT IT IS MY
CHIEF DUTY TO ACCOMPLISH HUMBLE TASKS AS THOUGH THEY
WERE GREAT AND NOBLE.

THE WORLD IS MOVED ALONG, NOT ONLY BY THE MIGHTY
SHOVES OF ITS HEROES, BUT ALSO BY THE AGGREGATE OF THE
TINY PUSHES OF EACH HONEST WORKER.

—HELEN KELLER

You will recall that it was my "performance appraisal" meeting with Kelly in 1996 that ultimately influenced my decision to write a book about acknowledgment. You may also remember that as a result of Kelly's performance after the 30-Day Process, we never did get around to doing a "real" performance review because it was unnecessary.

The subject of the more traditional approach to performance reviews came up again when I was researching the competition for this book. Agents, editors, and publishers are always interested in knowing what sets any book apart from others that may be similar. Using the Internet, I logged on to Amazon.com and asked for a listing of all books written about "praising or acknowledging others."

The results of this search fell into two distinct categories: workplace performance reviews and "praising God." When I pulled up the list of books written about performance reviews, there were more than a hundred. I read synopses of those that seemed most closely related to my own topic. The recurring theme seemed to be how to give employees "just enough" praise to balance the "real" message of the review: that there were areas of performance and behavior that had better change for the better in the next year if continued employment and/or promotion were to remain options. In other words, praise or acknowledgment was more often than not used to soften the blow of the review's real purpose, which was pointing out areas of weakness where improvement was needed.

I was struck by this almost incidental insertion of acknowledgment into evaluating and improving employee performance. On the one hand, experts have told us for years that one of our greatest needs as humans is to be validated, to know that we matter. On the other hand, we behave as if meeting that need were subservient to fixing the parts of us (at least at work) that no longer seem to be functioning as well as they should.

This is even more puzzling when I consider how quick we are to buy into the notion that "the customer is always right." Now, any of us who has ever spent time in a service-driven organization knows that the customer is, in fact, not always right. But we need to interact with customers as if there were substance to their request, claim, argument, or point of view. And this advice seems to work pretty well.

So why wouldn't this same advice hold true for those we are asking to provide the service—for a coworker, client, vendor, customer, or constituent? What if managers inter-acted with their employees as if there were substance to their ideas and suggestions—in fact, to employees themselves? The prevailing mind-set seems to be "Prove to us that you're worthy and competent, and then we will treat you accord-ingly." What if our mind-set were one that *assumed from day one* that each employee is, in fact, worthy, competent, and deserving of our praise and acknowledgment for a job well done, day in and day out?

This would assume a high level of trust in the hiring process, an assumption that anyone who made it through the interviewing and hiring process is indeed worthy of employment in the organization. I remember hearing Horst Schulze, the CEO of the Ritz-Carlton, deliver an address some years ago in which he said that when an employee did not succeed in the company and had to be terminated, "it was the company's fault for not doing its job in the hiring process." Part of the Ritz-Carlton's mission statement says, "We are ladies and gentlemen serving ladies and gentlemen." According to Mr. Schulze, only ladies and gentlemen are hired; therefore, they are treated as such *from the first day of their employment.*

To many organizations this is a bizarre way of evaluating employees, i.e., holding the company responsible for what goes wrong. Some of those same organizations would also envy the loyalty, productivity, and service provided by Ritz-Carlton employees.

Three highly successful organizations profiled later in this book demonstrate what happens when employees are treated as ladies and gentlemen.

My focus here is not to suggest ways of creating a foolproof hiring process. Rather, I want to concentrate on organizations' responsibility, once good people are hired, to ensure that they feel valued and affirmed for their contributions.

While there are many random and incidental ways of acknowledging employees, let's examine an obvious (and sometimes abused) tool, the performance appraisal. *Merriam-Webster's New Twentieth Century Dictionary* tells us that the word "appraisal" means "to value; to esteem; to praise; to speak well of." This could be interpreted to mean that the purpose of performance appraisals is "to value, to esteem, to praise, and to speak well of" the performance of those being evaluated.

I was a part of the corporate environment for more than thirty years and have been on both the giving and receiving ends of performance appraisals for many of those years. I don't know about you, but my experience was rarely one of eager anticipation, whether I was the giver or the receiver. For the receivers, it was something to be dreaded, and for many managers charged with the responsibility, it was something to be avoided if possible. (Remember, I couldn't even bring myself to follow through with Kelly's more traditional performance review because I knew it was intended in part to break the bad news about what wasn't working.) I don't think the avoidance or dread is there because we fear being valued, esteemed, praised, or spoken well of. Rather, it is there because of the very absence of those things.

Performance appraisals are used, for the most part, to build a case for future negative action. They lay the ground rules for what will happen "if." They are part of the neces-sary documentation "in case." No matter how praiseworthy they start out, "waiting for the other shoe to drop" seems to be an integral part of the agenda.

At this point I want to interject that I am not an oppo-nent of performance appraisals. Properly used, they provide a useful and structured opportunity for both the receiver and the giver to assess what's working and what's not. It's the "properly used" qualification that needs a bit of work.

For example, managers who do not consistently and reg-ularly let their employees know how they are doing tend to store up any concerns they may have and then dump them all at once during a performance appraisal. In such situa-tions, employees may learn for the first time that something they did several months ago is now a cause for concern by their boss. In other words, a performance appraisal may be nothing more than a formalized way of delivering bad news that should have been shared along the way.

Inserting a complimentary phrase here and there does lit-tle to balance the barrage of a year's worth of performance misgivings stored up by managers. In such situations, "bal-ance" would mean that those same managers had also stored up everything praiseworthy about an employee for a year as well and were now using the performance appraisal to release a barrage of good news. But in fact, when praise is handed out in this manner, it feels less like acknowledgment than a setup.

For example, one employer who decided to do the 30-Day Process with a valued coworker started out by sharing one quality a day. This lasted about ten days. Then nothing happened until the thirtieth day, when the employer lumped twenty traits together, put them in writing, and left the list on the employee's desk. The coworker revealed that those last twenty traits felt less like acknowledgment and more like a frantic attempt to complete the process on time.

It was never the intention that performance appraisals should be used as a backstop for managerial ineffectiveness. That they have gravitated toward this end only gives credibility to the surveys that show that our greatest need at work is to feel valued and appreciated (and that we leave when we don't).

A vice president of a major health care organization decided to do the 30-Day Process with her assistant. She—and her assistant—was so pleased with the outcome that she said to me, "You know, we should really change performance appraisals into performance 'praisals' for our employees. I think a lot more would get done if we started praising them regularly."

I like her idea. Here's my suggestion.

Use the 30-Day Process to help you get into the habit of paying attention—very careful attention—to the contributions of those you count on at work (as well as at home and in the community). Use the process to correct your blurred vision when it comes to noticing and acknowledging what people around you are doing. Notice who they are as individuals as well as what job functions they perform. The very best kind of acknowledgment is that which affirms who we are intrinsically as well as what we do.

For example, if you know that an employee is actively involved in the lives of his or her children, acknowledge that person for being a great parent. I can assure you that the devotion given to a child is also available to be given to a task or job. If someone is slow to judge and quick to embrace all points of view, tell that person how much you value this objectivity and generosity of spirit. If an employee works tirelessly with few complaints, praise that person's tenacity and compassion. The part of a person that is compassionate, generous of spirit, and giving to others is as essential to extraordinary performance as is the mastery of certain skills.

Pay attention to who the people are who show up day after day and perform their jobs in a way that helps the company move forward. All of us want to be honored for who we are as well as what we do. Most performance appraisals are designed or used to comment on what others *do*. I recommend that you consciously include some time to comment on who they *are* as well.

In more courageous organizations, performance "praisals" can become a stand-alone resource, a time set aside specifically and exclusively for the purpose of honoring and acknowledging individuals for their contributions. Knowing that we are going to be praised would give us little reason to dread such a meeting. In fact, such a meeting might just render the dread of the more traditional performance review unnecessary.

As I found in my experience with Kelly, if you give people a positive image of themselves, they tend to do everything possible to live up to it. When we behave in alignment with such images—the ones that celebrate who we are—performance problems diminish and productivity soars. In the workshops I conduct on this topic, managers and non-managers alike comment on what happens when they feel validated:

- They take ownership of the organization's success.
- They experience less stress and less burnout.
- Turnover decreases and loyalty increases.
- Productivity and creativity increase.
- Open communication leads to early warning of potential problems.
- Humor is used to nurture, not to diminish.

Some organizations only dream of a workforce that operates in this manner. These are the same organizations that want results without having to put forth effort. One employer commented to me that he "shouldn't have to coddle his employees to get peak performance." I suggest that if acknowledgment is perceived as coddling, peak performance will always remain elusive.

So what about taking on the initiative of performance "praisals"? As Chapter 9 showed, there are dozens of ways to make acknowledgment a part of the workplace culture. Just remember that short-term efforts and random topic-of-the-month approaches produce short-term results. Long-term, sustainable results come only when the level of commitment, compassion, and curiosity is high; when employees are praised for who they are as individuals, not just as people who perform well within the confines of a job description.

Setting aside a specific time and place for performance "praisals" can be one of the best investments a company makes. Whether it is done once a day or once a week, the key is to have it be ongoing. I like the idea of using the 30-Day Process to jump-start such initiatives because it does a wonderful job of teaching us the *habit* of acknowledgment.

For those of you who may be wondering what a performance "praisal" might be, ask your employees what would make them feel validated and valued for their work. Tell them you would like to be more active in praising their contributions. Let them tell you what they're doing on a regular basis that they feel is worthy of acknowledgment. You will be surprised to find that it is the common, everyday tasks done well for which most people seek recognition.

Managers tend to reserve their praise for spectacular accomplishments: meeting a tough deadline, coming in under budget, and so on. While such achievements are worthy of comment and praise, it is who employees are and what they do day in and day out that enables them to achieve some of the more noticeable results. The fact that an employee has shown up and done his or her job with little or no absenteeism year after year is worthy of mentioning on a regular basis: "I appreciate the fact that, no matter what, we can count on you to be here. That means a lot to the success of our business and to me personally."

Many employers think that if they don't have bonuses or prizes to hand out, there's little reason to praise someone's performance. Time after time, employees tell us that if they had to choose between a gift certificate or prize and regular recognition for their efforts, they would choose the verbal pat on the back every time.

Another suggestion is to include performance appraisals and performance "praisals" in the same document. Most organizations use some kind of standardized form to evaluate an employee's performance. Why not add a section to the form that speaks specifically to who that person is; a place to list the qualities, virtues, and principles that are intrinsic to that person and distinguish him or her from everyone else? Then, every time you see that person exhibiting those qualities or behaviors in the workplace, point them out and thank him or her.

So far our focus in this book has been primarily on what happens in the workplace when recognition and acknowledgment are part of the culture. It is also true that such initiatives can just as easily begin outside company walls, as the next chapter explains.

CHAPTER ELEVEN

SOMETIMES THE BEST PLACE TO BEGIN IS AT HOME

ONE MAN CANNOT DO RIGHT IN ONE DEPARTMENT OF LIFE WHILE HE IS OCCUPIED DOING WRONG IN ANY OTHER DEPARTMENT. LIFE IS ONE INDIVISIBLE WHOLE.
—MAHATMA GANDHI

For the most part, this book focuses on the need for acknowledgment as a workplace priority. After all, it was during an office performance review that the idea for this book originated. Also, as mentioned, lack of acknowledgment in the workplace is one of the main reasons employees voluntarily leave their jobs. For this reason it is appropriate to urge organizations to take the lead in creating more affirming cultures in which job satisfaction soars, productivity increases, and the world outside work becomes a better place in which to live.

The good news about creating an affirming workplace culture is that it impacts our home life as well. It's almost impossible not to feel good about being validated at work without taking that feeling home with you. If you are someone who by nature or habit is acknowledging, that attribute is not confined to your place of work but permeates all your relationships. For those of us who were fortunate enough to grow up in families where we were constantly praised and validated, it is hard for us *not* to praise others, whether at work or at home.

If you are not someone who works in an environment where you feel acknowledged and appreciated and you feel reluctant to start any kind of process of acknowledgment, perhaps the place for you to begin is at home or with your friends. Regardless of where you start, it will impact all areas of your life. Many of those who have tried the 30-Day Process started with a friend or family member and let it spread from there. Trust me when I say that when you feel the tremendous surge of energy that comes from being on the giving or receiving end of the 30-Day Process, that energy will be transported from the workplace to home and vice versa.

In this chapter, I want to share some success stories about people who started the 30-Day Process outside the workplace with a friend or family member.

Consider what happened when my husband, Tom, wanted to do the 30-Day Process with his son, Brad, a captain in the army who at the time was stationed in South Korea. Because of the geographic distance and time differences that separate them, as well as Brad's schedule, which has him "in the field" more often than not, Tom elected to do the process with him via e-mail—not as preferable and effective as doing it face-to-face but seemingly the best method in this situation. Here are some of Brad's comments about the impact of being affirmed:

Some of the things he's said have given me pause for thought in a positive light. One of the things Dad talked about was his seeing me as a "patriot." Honestly, no one's ever called me that to my face. When I read it, it didn't register at first, but about a day later, the thought occurred like this: someone finally acknowledged one of the dearest, most deeply held beliefs I have. Someone finally said, in essence, you believe in America enough to be willing to put your life on the line, if necessary. And that's a good thing about you.

That's the compliment that matters most to a soldier. Yes, the Army as an institution has its own system of rewards in the form of colored ribbons you put on your dress uniform. But I can swear that all of us, from general to the newest private freshly graduated from basic training, would trade all of our medals and accolades for the feeling a soldier gets when an ordinary American civilian walks up and sincerely says, "Thank you for doing what you do/did." Dad's simple acknowledgment of me as a patriot reconfirmed for me why I put up with the trials of command.

Although he's never used these exact words, I think Tom really does sleep better at night knowing that the U.S. Army counts on people like Brad.

Another compelling story is about a friend who decided to do the 30-Day Process with her forty-year-old son, who had suffered a head injury almost twelve years earlier. As a result of the injury, he lived in a group home with others who are learning to function with similar limitations. For a variety of reasons, he was angry and bitter, and much of this was directed toward his mother. When she would go to visit, he would sometimes refuse to see her or behave rudely if they went out for lunch or dinner, to the embarrassment of both his mother and others in the restaurant.

His mother thought the 30-Day Process might soften some of the sharper edges of their relationship.

When this friend first told me she wanted to do the 30-Day Process with her son and explained the circumstances, I warned her that the unusual circumstances under which she wanted to try the process might not produce the same results. She persisted, and the lesson was mine to learn.

She wrote out each of her son's good qualities on three-by-five-inch cards and mailed them to him. She acknowledged him for the simple things he could do: make his bed, keep the kitchen clean, adapt to his new circumstances, say a kind word to others, and so on. The mother commented that it was good to focus on all of his wonderful qualities rather than the anger that divided them. Shortly after starting the process, she began to see changes in him. He was eager for her to visit and insisted that they go out to eat. His behavior was exemplary.

She started to see him in a different light, because he started to see himself that way as well.

I am almost reluctant to include this touching story about this mother and her son because my belief is that what happened is probably an exception. The 30-Day Process was not intended to be tried in such unusual circumstances. But this mother is extraordinary, and I share her story because I was—and am—so moved by what happened.

I was also moved by the story of a friend who did the 30-Day Process with her husband. She said that during the course of identifying his positive traits, she started to fall in love with him all over again. She concluded her feedback form by saying, "I felt really special to have attracted such a wonderful man as my husband. Our relationship has never been better."

Another woman who did the process with her significant other said that the process had helped shift her focus about him. She wrote, "It is easy to fixate on a few annoying characteristics and lose sight of who he really is. I realized what a perfect companion he is for me. Had I seen the list of his traits without knowing him, I would have wanted to meet him and get to know him." She concluded her feedback form by saying, "I saw an eagerness on his part to receive his daily trait. It seemed like nourishment to him. He glowed. I believe he was disappointed when the thirty days were over, almost as though he had stopped taking a daily vitamin!"

A similar insight was noted by another spouse who did the process with her husband. She admitted that her tendency had been to focus on what *didn't* work about him and often to be critical of his behavior. She said the 30-Day Process had provided the balance her view of him had been missing. The mirroring impact of the process was also in evidence. This wife concluded by saying, "I realized that both of us possessed the qualities I was sharing with him. It made both of us feel more special about who we had selected as life partners."

A former work colleague elected to do the 30-Day Process with his fifteen-year-old daughter. This father's definition of a family was "a place where one is loved and safe." He wanted his daughter to know how much she was loved, so he thought the 30-Day Process would be a way of accomplishing this. He said that his greatest insight had been realizing that while he frequently gave her compliments, his "genuineness and sincerity needed to be examined." He went on to say, "I watched her grow in self-esteem and a feeling of security in our family. As a result of the process, our relationship has grown more solid, stable, and deep. It pleased her to know that I was looking for things to like and enjoy about her."

One of my favorite success stories with the 30-Day Process occurred between a grandmother-in-law and her grandson-in-law. That this was my (then) eighty-five-year-old mother doing the process with my own son-in-law made it all the more poignant. She confessed that her grandson-in-law's initial response to her offer to do the process with him was that she probably couldn't think of that many good things to say about him. After all, their relationship was primarily confined to seeing each other on holidays and at other occasional family gatherings. How well could she know him? But she did. She called him every day and shared a trait. Occasionally, when she was later than usual in calling him, he would call her! This thrilled her. Needless to say, family ties were strengthened all around.

Speaking of this (now) eighty-seven-year-old mother, when I was doing the 30-Day Process with her, one of the things I praised her for was remaining youthful and open to new ideas. A great example of that is going on even as I write these words.

My daughter Kelly Newman, who now owns a ComputerMoms franchise in Dallas, volunteers her services one day a week at the retirement community where my mother lives, helping senior citizens learn to navigate the Internet and communicate with friends and family via e-mail. My mother at first insisted that where computers are concerned, she definitely qualified as an old dog who could not learn a new trick. Nonetheless, she faithfully went to the classes Kelly taught. After only a few weeks, she decided she wanted her own computer (and printer!) and had Kelly order them for her. Is it any wonder that I acknowledged her for having an openness to new ideas?

Another comment from a 30-Day Process participant I especially enjoyed came from a woman whose partner became more and more excited each time she shared a trait. It got to the point where her partner greeted her at the door at night by asking, "What's special about me today?" The spouse commented on her feedback form, "I think I've created a [acknowledgment] monster—and I love every bit of it!"

Speaking of creating a monster, I want to share part of my story of when I did the process with my husband. By the time I asked Tom if I could do the 30-Day Process with him, he was very familiar with the routine, having heard me talk about my experiences with my daughters and others. His initial response to my request was to roll his eyes, sigh heavily, and reluctantly agree. His body language was saying, "I don't really need this stuff, but I don't know a cool way to get out of it."

The first few traits I shared with him were not surprises. For the most part, he knew that these were qualities I admired about him. He did seem to enjoy the specific examples I offered for each trait. As the days passed, he became more and more ready and willing to hear his trait for the day. I usually shared a trait with him each night before we went to sleep. One night, after an especially long and draining day, I commented to Tom as I crawled into bed that I was really tired and could probably fall asleep in ten seconds. His response? "Will you share a trait with me first?"

Finally, I want to share what another friend and former business associate did to acknowledge her two children. She listed each of their qualities on a card that was posted on the kitchen refrigerator. Whenever she saw her children exhibiting one of these qualities, she would point it out to them so they would have a clear understanding of what these virtues look like in action. Her kids seemed eager to model the traits and would say things like "Am I doing it now, Mom?" Not a bad way of building the self-esteem of which children are so deserving.

I share these stories because I would like you to begin the process of acknowledgment wherever it works best for you. If a friend or family member seems to be the logical place to begin, I applaud that decision.

We tend to act out at work whatever is going on at home, and vice versa. It really doesn't matter whether or not your decision to be more direct in affirming those who mean the most to you begins at home, in the community where you live, or at work. Sooner or later, all those areas will feel the impact of your commitment.

CHAPTER TWELVE

THE "LOWE" DOWN ON TDINDUSTRIES

THERE ARE NO TRICKS TO BECOMING A GOOD PLACE TO WORK,
JUST A TOP-TO-BOTTOM, ROCK-RIBBED BELIEF THAT EVERYBODY
IN THE COMPANY COUNTS THE SAME.
— JACK LOWE, JR., CEO, TDINDUSTRIES

In January of each year *Fortune* magazine announces its list of the "100 Best Companies to Work For." Three of the top six companies listed for 2000 are based in Dallas, and two of those companies are next-door neighbors. The Container Store and TDIndustries are far apart in the nature of their businesses but neck and neck when it comes to celebrating the achievements of their employees.

The first step in applying for *Fortune*'s "100 Best" list is to submit a two-page letter explaining why the company should be considered for the list. The approximately 200-plus finalists (out of approximately 1,000 applicants) are then required to distribute a Trust Index, created by the Great Place to Work Institute, to 250 employees selected at random. More than any other national survey of companies, the *Fortune* "100 Best" list is employee-driven, with two-thirds of the scoring based on the answers employees give.

The Container Store entered this competition for the first time in 1999 and was named the number one company on the list, an unheard-of accomplishment for a first-time applicant. TDIndustries has been in the top six of the *Fortune* "100 Best" for four consecutive years.

It is for these reasons that, in this chapter and the next, the Container Store and TDIndustries are profiled as extraordinary models of workplace environments where acknowledgment is a high priority.

Let's begin our company profiles with TDIndustries.

TDIndustries is a Dallas-based business that installs and services commercial air-conditioning and plumbing equipment. The construction industry is a sharply competitive environment, and TD works hard to maintain its position as one of the top mechanical and service companies in Texas and the twelfth largest in the nation. George Liles was working at TDIndustries in July 2000, when cancer claimed his life only a few weeks after his initial diagnosis. George was fifty-five. When word spread throughout the company about George's illness, TD responded as only TD can do.

George's work colleagues started showing up at his home daily to bring food, to visit, and to tend to any needs he and his family might have. This included finishing some plumbing work in his bathroom that he had started before his illness; it also included repairing the air conditioning twice before finally replacing the condenser. A young man whom George had mentored replaced the locks on the doors, another unfinished project. All of this was done at

TD's expense, including parts.

The president, CEO, and other senior officers of the company all visited George at his home. Jack Lowe, Jr., TD's CEO, visited George for several hours on a Sunday morning before leaving town on a business trip. George's message to his team at work was to let them know he was "sorry I'm not there helping you."

These things were done for George because he was a good guy who never said no to any assignment. He did what he was asked to do, including taking a one-year assignment in Houston to work for a TD client there, commuting on weekends to be with his family.

Many companies would show similar compassion and generosity for one of their own, especially those at the more senior levels of the company and with long years of service. George was neither. He had been employed at TD for less than ten years when he died. His job? Plumbing superintendent (which, incidentally, at TD qualified him for all four levels of leadership training, three of which he had completed at the time of his death).

When I interviewed George's boss, Ben Simmons, who delivered the eulogy at George's funeral, I asked him what his official title at TD was. He responded, "My business card says 'vice president,' but I prefer you to say that I am a team leader." This is indicative of how even the most senior people at TDIndustries see themselves—as servant leaders.

By the way, when it was time for George Liles to have his picture taken on the occasion of his fifth anniversary with the company, he insisted on wearing his hard hat.

Hard hats make up 90 percent of the workforce, not typical of most of the companies that make *Fortune*'s "100 Best Companies to Work For" list.

TDIndustries has ranked in the top six on *Fortune*'s list for four consecutive years. The last question on *Fortune*'s survey of TD's employees asked, "Taking all things into account, is this a great place to work?"

Ninety-five percent answered yes; only 5 percent said no.

TD's CEO, Jack Lowe, Jr., responded to those results with the same humility his coworkers say he brings to work every day. At a party to celebrate making the list of the best companies to work for, Jack told his people, "We need to be proud about this but with a good dose of humility. As long as we've got one person who doesn't think this is a great place to work, we've got work to do."

Jack grew up with the company started by his father in 1946. He attributes TD's success to its people-first philosophy, based on an idea called "servant leadership," outlined in a book by the same title authored by Robert Greenleaf. Mr. Greenleaf was a Quaker businessman who worked in personnel at AT&T. He wrote an essay in the 1960s entitled "The Servant as Leader," based on the notion that leaders exist to serve those who work for them.

Jack's version of this philosophy is summed up this way: "It's simply that the role of leadership is to serve, and the test is whether people grow. That's what underlies what we do. The reason we're in this business is to provide outstanding career opportunities. Of course, we can't do that unless we're blowing away our competitors. Do all those things, and the money just takes care of itself."

But the money did not always take care of itself. In the

late 1980s, the Dallas economy went into free fall when oil prices collapsed, and the state's real estate and banking industries went down as well. Construction projects were few and far between. Senior management at TD tried to out-run what was happening in Texas by bidding on jobs in other states. While aggressive bidding won the company a lot of contracts, most of the out-of-state projects ran into sig-nificant cost overruns. At the height of the crisis the com-pany lost 40 percent of its net worth.

The company's bank had failed, and investors were nowhere to be found. The immediate challenge of raising enough cash to hold off creditors was met when the com-pany's three top officers staked their homes as personal guarantees to the bonding company insuring the company's projects.

But the company needed much more help.

This is where the servant leadership approach paid big dividends. Jack called a meeting that all employees with more than five years of service were invited to attend. The company's pension plan was overfunded by $1 million, and the employees, asked to give the money back to the com-pany, voted to do so. Then, in what Jack describes as an act of extraordinary courage, the employees contributed an additional $1.25 million out of their retirement fund in exchange for company stock.

Considering the shape of the construction industry at the time, this was a high-risk investment. (Those shares have since tripled in value.)

Jack's response? "The way I think about it, it's just the old we're-in-this-together deal." He meant what he said since

TDIndustries is owned by its employees. Today about 25 percent of the stock is held by the top thirty managers of the company, with Jack Lowe, Jr., holding only 5 percent. The other 75 percent of the stock is held by nonmanagement employees.

When Jack's father first began to sell stock to the company's employees, it was as a quick way of raising working capital without going into debt. But it also fit his vision that management and workers ought to be partners. To this day, you won't hear employees distinguished as "managers" or "workers." Everyone is called a "partner."

One of those partners, a piping foreman who has been with the company seven years, says, "I've never felt more welcome at a company or worked anywhere where my opinion meant something. This is the only job I've had where I've wanted to stay more than two years."

Another partner, Jessie McCain, puts it this way: "It doesn't take a person very long to realize something is a little different here." Jessie came to TD in 1980, just after turning forty and disillusioned after a divorce. "I mistrusted everyone," she says. Jessie started at the bottom of the human resources department at $6.50 an hour; she's now its vice president. "Jack gave my life back to me. I needed a chance, and Jack gave that to me. He believed in me more than I believed in myself."

Jessie's experience meshes with Jack's response when asked what he considered to be his best asset: "My belief in people's ability to be great if given the chance."

The walls at TD's offices are lined with pictures of employees cited for their long years of service. These walls surround rows and rows of . . . cubicles. Yep, there are no private offices at TDIndustries. At its north Dallas headquarters, there are two sizes of cubicles: eight by eight feet and eight by eleven feet. Because of his rank in the company, Jack Lowe, Jr., the CEO, has one of the larger cubicles. The parking lot out front also has no reserved spaces for executives.

This physical openness sets the tone for Jack's open style of leadership. Any employee knows that he or she can, at any time, talk to Jack about a problem or issue of concern. In fact, Jack makes a point of talking to every employee personally for three hours every two years. Robert Levering, the coauthor of the *Fortune* survey, says, "A lot of CEOs have people react to them with almost fear and awe. This is just absolutely, totally not true with him. He is very straightforward and down to earth."

My own experience with TDIndustries started in the early 1990s, when I was working with the Covey Leadership Center. TD was putting its partners through a training program based on Stephen Covey's book *The Seven Habits of Highly Effective People.* Before the book's huge success, Dr. Covey himself taught the "Seven Habits" classes at TD. I had the good fortune to succeed Dr. Covey in facilitating those classes, and I continue to do so. I, too, learned quickly that there was something very, very different about TDIndustries.

For starters, when I arrived in the training classroom one morning, one of the custodial partners was still setting up the room. The training coordinator was also in the room. Upon seeing me she immediately said, "Oh, Dottie, I'm so glad you're here early enough to meet one of our valued TD partners," and she proceeded to introduce by name the man setting up the room. She went on to say, "We don't know what we would do without him at TD. He helps make sure that everything runs smoothly by ensuring that all of our meeting rooms are inviting when the people arrive."

I seriously doubt that the custodial staff in other organizations is treated with the same respect and dignity as this man.

Most companies teaching the "Seven Habits" generally send managers and top executives to the program. At TD, however, in addition to top management (all of whom completed the training first as a model to employees), the classes are filled with the rank and file, the hard-hat population that makes up most of the company's employees. When employees are selected to participate in the program, they are told that their selection was based on the company's belief in them as its future leaders.

Every class is introduced by one of the company's senior executives, and every class is closed by one of those same executives. These executives stress the importance of training at TD. What makes the classes even more impressive is that most of the participants are pulled off work sites for two days to participate in the training. Over and over again, I have heard employers say that it is too costly to pull the rank and file off their jobs to send them to training—not so at TDIndustries.

And it's not just two days of "Seven Habits" training that these workers participate in. "Seven Habits" is one of a four-part leadership series that all these employees attend. This kind of investment in training sends a powerful message to employees—namely, that they matter, their opinions count, and the company values them.

While there have been a few disappointments over the years, Jack Lowe, Jr., has never stopped trusting the employees at TD. "Being a servant leader doesn't mean being a sap. There's a lot of tough love. When problems sometimes arise, one impulse is to put the hammer down and tighten up. But the cost of telling a bunch of people 'We don't trust you' is so much higher than the occasional slip."

It is just that kind of acknowledgment that results in very few slips at TDIndustries.

CHAPTER THIRTEEN

THE BEST PLACE TO GET ORGANIZED IS ALSO THE BEST PLACE TO WORK

A FUNNY THING HAPPENS WHEN YOU TAKE THE TIME TO EDUCATE YOUR EMPLOYEES, PAY THEM WELL, AND TREAT THEM AS EQUALS. YOU END UP WITH EXTREMELY MOTIVATED AND ENTHUSIASTIC PEOPLE.

—KIP TINDELL, CEO AND COFOUNDER, THE CONTAINER STORE

In addition to TDIndustries, two other Dallas-based companies made the top 10 on *Fortune*'s "100 Best" list for 2000. One of the two, Southwest Airlines, came as no surprise—it has ranked high on the list every year since its inception. The other company, the Container Store, came as more of a surprise as 2000 was the first year it had entered the competition—and it took the top honor! And then retained its number one ranking in 2001!

In 1978, the Container Store originated the retail category of storage and organization with one mission: to offer its customers, through impeccable customer service, innovative products that save them precious time and space. The company now has twenty stores across the country as well as a prosperous national mail-order service, and it has developed a culture in which its more than 1,500 employees can thrive while embracing the company's "do unto others" business philosophy.

In addition to taking great care of its customers, the Container Store takes great care of its employees. In an industry that averages about seven hours of training for first-year, full-time employees, the Container Store offers *235 hours*. This training and the high level of communication within the company have been cited as factors in its low turnover rate, which has historically been 15 to 25 percent. The industry average is more than 100 percent.

The company also pays its employees much more than its competitors do, shares daily sales information with employees, and offers sabbaticals after ten years on the job.

As one of the Container Store's highly satisfied customers (my home office in which this book is being written was completely furnished by the Container Store, from desk and shelving to storage areas), I was interested in learning more about its culture. Shortly after TDIndustries and the Container Store were named winners on *Fortune*'s "100 Best" list for 1999, I was invited by TDIndustries to hear a presentation by Garrett Boone and Kip Tindell, the cofounders of the Container Store. TD and the Container Store are across-the-street neighbors, so TD had invited Garrett and Kip to share their story with the employees and friends of TDIndustries.

It didn't take much listening to conclude that the Container Store is a remarkable model when it comes to valuing and affirming its employees. Following the presentation, I asked Kip if he would grant me an interview for this book. He did.

When I arrived at company headquarters for the interview, there was another woman in the reception area who was there for a follow-up job interview. Kip Tindell bounded into the waiting area, wearing blue jeans and a sweatshirt, and greeted both of us enthusiastically. He asked the other woman if she was being "well taken care of." She responded, "Yes," and he proceeded to ask her what she thought about her interviews with the Container Store so far (Kip being one of those who had already interviewed her). She said she was favorably impressed and was looking forward to her additional interviews that morning. Kip told her, "We really like you. We hope you'll like us, too." She smiled in response.

Kip then turned to me, and we were starting up the stairs to his office for our interview when he suddenly stopped, turned again to the other woman, and said quite excitedly, "Well, what do you really think? Do we have a chance with you?" This time she laughed and said he would know soon enough, after the rest of her interviews.

I later realized during our interview that what I had witnessed was not the impulsive action of an overeager executive but an intentional part of the hiring philosophy at the Container Store.

Kip says, "Our people are easy to acknowledge because we hire such good people. This happens because we *believe* we can attract them. Many companies say they have our same philosophy about hiring good people, but we really believe and act on it." This is born out by the fact that the Container Store has never in its twenty-two-year history placed a classified ad for employees and says it never will. During these same twenty-two years, the Container Store has lost only three key executives, this in spite of the fact that its people are bombarded with calls from headhunters. Part of the Container Store's hiring philosophy is to keep all positions filled and good people waiting in the wings. This became a lot easier following the announcement of its number one listing by *Fortune,* when it was so swamped with applications for employment that key people had to be pulled off other assignments to assist in handling the overflow.

I was interested to learn that many of the company's employees come from its large supply of satisfied customers. Employees are encouraged to hand out "gold cards" to friendly customers. These business-card sized invitations say simply, "The most organized store in America is looking for a few neat people," and then gives a phone number. Some customers-turned-employees say they had no intention of going to work or going back to work. Nonetheless, intrigued by this approach, many have inquired, and many have been hired. Kip says, "A satisfied customer makes a great employee for us."

While most retailers keep "now hiring" signs permanently posted at their work locations, the Container Store never seems to be in short supply of the "few neat people" it wants for its positions.

So when exactly do employees discover that they are working for a company that values and honors their contributions? It begins with their very first interview. Kip says, "We overinterview. We convey up front how excited we are to have this person working with us. We want them to know we'll do everything we can to make their experience with us a good one." (Thus the interaction I witnessed in the reception area.)

Once hired, employees are put through what Kip calls "perspective training." "We don't want anyone to feel that they are left dangling out there. Employees hired into management spend lots of time with *all* our top people. We want everyone who comes to work for us to feel safe, secure, warm. We provide unbelievable support because we want everyone to succeed."

From the very beginning, employees sense that they have come to work for a great organization that believes very strongly in their individual success. It is also important for employees to understand that they are part of a team. "Teaming is one of life's most beautiful experiences," Kip believes.

The Container Store wants its employees to love and respect the products they sell. Kip likens the relationship between employee and product to that of an impressionist painting that "transcends value." He wants the company's products to work so well for the customers that employees become emotional about them.

"Our purpose at headquarters is to do everything we can for the people in our stores." That's one of the reasons the company provides 235 hours of training for its first-year full-time employees. This level of training also allows customers to feel as if they're dealing with a manager, regardless of the person's position in the store. In order for this to happen, says Kip, "we believe in unshackling our employees so they are freed up to do more."

This is in sharp contrast to organizations that believe that strict controls and detailed work rules are the best way of making sure employees don't foul up. The Container Store focuses on helping employees succeed, not on preventing them from fouling up.

This company also has a rather unusual philosophy as to how some of its people are paid. The retail industry is not one noted for high wages, yet the Container Store pays 50 to 100 percent above the industry average, *except for its top executives*. Although senior executives are paid well, they are not paid 50 to 100 percent above the industry average.

The rationale for paying good rank-and-file employees double what the company's competitors may offer is based on a productivity mind-set that goes something like this:

- One average employee does the work of three lousy employees.
- One good employee does the work of three average employees.
- One great employee does the work of three good employees.

This model turns out to be a winning approach for everyone.

- The company wins because it hires great employees, pays them up to double the going rate, and gets three times the productivity.
- The employee wins because he or she is paid up to twice what the competition pays.
- Customers win because they have a great person to help them at the store.

Kip admits that it takes "courage and bravery" to pay people well in his industry. That this courage has paid off is attested to by the large numbers of people waiting to be employed by the Container Store.

Kip Tindell and Garrett Boone spend a lot of time interacting with their people, chatting with employees and customers, asking them what they need, and getting their opinions and input on new products and ideas. "You can't tell people enough how much you appreciate them. It's important to us that our people know how we feel about them," Kip told me.

When I asked Kip how he would sum up his approach to this kind of affirming leadership, he said it was "grace of authority." He believes that people in positions of authority should behave with grace. He mentioned the actor Jimmy Stewart as an example of grace with authority and Napoleon as someone who was not graceful with his authority.

At the TDIndustries meeting I attended, where I first met Kip Tindell and Garrett Boone, one of the attendees asked them what would happen to someone, say a store manager, who did not honor the grace of authority. "Well," Garrett said, "they just wouldn't do that." He could recall only one manager during the company's long history who had been let go because of a misuse of authority.

As with all great companies where acknowledgment is a priority, the Container Store is not content to rest on its laurels. When Kip and Garrett first learned that their company had been ranked number one on *Fortune*'s "100 Best" list, their response included an acknowledgment of their employees:

Being selected as the top company on Fortune's list is such a dream for all of us, and we'd like to thank all of our employees for making The Container Store a special place to work. The honor is truly a motivation to make something great even greater—it is a never-ending journey for us.

CHAPTER FOURTEEN

LIVING AND WORKING IN A STATE OF "GRACE"

WE ARE WHAT WE REPEATEDLY DO.
EXCELLENCE, THEN, IS NOT AN ACT, BUT A HABIT.
    —ARISTOTLE

Tom and I are blessed to have three out of our four parents alive and relatively healthy, in spite of their ages, which at this writing range from eighty-seven to ninety-one years. Several years ago, faced with the task of finding a senior care facility for them, we were delighted to discover Grace Presbyterian Village in south Dallas. Tom's parents moved in first, and my parents followed about a year later. (My father died about two years after moving there.)

Grace Presbyterian Village is a thirty-eight-year-old, nonprofit Texas corporation that provides housing, health care, and other programs and services for older adults. Established in 1962 in the Oak Cliff section of Dallas, Grace Presbyterian Village is a covenant mission partner with Grace Presbytery of the Presbyterian Church but is nonsectarian in its admission policy. The village is in a campuslike setting, with winding trails, many mature trees, and a lovely creek that winds its way through the campus.

Although my husband and I were appreciative of the level of care our parents received in the beginning, there was high staff turnover, fluctuating morale, and the usual politics that go with the running of a nonprofit facility. My husband was elected to the board of directors and soon shared the concern of several other members regarding the lack of effective leadership at the village. This concern eventually led to a change at the top. That change came in the form of the arrival of Godwin Dixon, who, in September 1999, assumed the role of executive director of the village. Things haven't been the same since.

When I first heard him share his vision for Grace Presbyterian Village in a public forum, I was struck by the simplicity of his message: "If you make the people who work with you feel appreciated and valued, all of what we want for this place will happen." Period. That was it.

Intrigued with this philosophy, I asked Godwin if he would agree to an interview for this book. He readily consented, and I found myself amazed at what he shared with me. His story was so impressive, so touching, that I decided on the spot to use Godwin and Grace Presbyterian Village as a case study of what's possible in a nonprofit environment when acknowledgment is a priority.

Thus, the third organization to be profiled is Grace Presbyterian Village in Dallas, Texas.

In the early part of his career, Godwin started out as a nurse's aide in a nursing care facility where few bothered to know one another by name, nor was that viewed as necessary. Monthly staff meetings were held for the purpose of telling people what they were doing wrong. Then when a new administrator arrived on the scene, he immediately started thanking everyone for their contributions. "Because there was a shift in how we were seen, there was also a shift in how we saw ourselves and others," Godwin said. The new administrator sought the opinions of line staff, something previously unheard of. Godwin says this man became his role model for how a manager could run an organization.

Eventually, Godwin himself became the administrator of a two-hundred-bed nursing home in Houston. When he arrived, the facility was one step away from being shut down by the state for a variety of violations. The *Houston Chronicle* called the facility "one of the worst in the State of Texas."

Immediately upon arrival, Godwin made himself visible on all of the floors of the facility, greeting people and making a point of learning everyone's name. He constantly told the staff how much he appreciated what they were doing. He told me how much the staff had appreciated it when he would bring a box of chicken wings to the evening shift as a thank-you for their hard work. "It cost me about five dollars, but the payoffs were much larger."

At one point he made a decision to give plaques to deserving staff members. While someone in Godwin's position is used to receiving plaques for various reasons, line staff are usually excluded from this kind of recognition. "Giving plaques to these folks may cost a little more," noted Godwin, "but the effect is huge."

He was especially impressed with the dietary staff at this facility, who had managed to stay together for more than ten years during some "horrible" times. Because this was a Medicaid facility, staffing was generally insufficient, and the budget allowed only $2.63 a day per resident for all three meals. In spite of this, the dietary department "cranked out good meals and did so within budget." Godwin had a plaque engraved for this group, commending their exceptional service and commitment. Every member of the dietary staff had his or her name engraved on the plaque, *including some who had retired before Godwin's arrival.*

That plaque became a source of great pride and a reason to come to work. These people wanted to work where they had been recognized. Staff members daily pointed to their names with pride.

When Godwin left that facility in 1992, the plaques were still on the wall. He had occasion to return there in 1997, and while the plaques he had made were still there, none had been added or hung since then. (Nor had any been given prior to his arrival there.) As Godwin put it, "I would think that subsequent administrators would either have wanted to continue that tradition or, barring that, would at least have taken the plaques down. As it stands, the message those plaques convey now is that there was a point in time when staff were publicly acknowledged for their contributions, and now they are not. To my way of thinking, it is a glaring and unfortunate reminder of what is no longer done."

Godwin also paid attention to the staff break room. He wanted it to convey a feeling of truly being a place to take a break from the duties of work. He made certain that there was a working refrigerator as well as other amenities the staff had requested. No longer was it a run-down and uninviting place in which to rest.

He also instituted an Adopt a Resident program; staff members were allowed to wear special T-shirts on Fridays, when they assumed the roles of adoptive family to the residents.

Godwin let the staff know that he would ask nothing of them that he would not be willing to do himself. He was not reluctant to pick trash up off the floor, tidy up areas that needed it, and even feed residents and give them baths when the staff was shorthanded. The staff also knew that if they had a difficult patient, they could go directly to Godwin for assistance.

Staff meetings at this facility also underwent a turnaround after Godwin's arrival. No doubt he remembered the staff meetings in his earlier career, where people had been told only what they were doing wrong. At this facility he made a point of having the meetings be positive. He would always start the meetings by thanking all those present for their hard work. Next he would cover any negatives or unpopular issues, but then he would end the meetings on a positive note. He would discuss positive issues and compliment staff on difficult problems that they had handled especially well. When he received letters from residents or their families thanking various staff members for their service, Godwin read them aloud at the staff meetings.

Another way he elected to care for those who worked there was to hold a candlelight vigil for staff who had family members then serving in the Persian Gulf War.

Although Godwin was at this facility for just two years, a complete turnaround in conditions occurred. Remember the state citations of the deficiencies at the facility when he arrived? During his tenure, the facility received its highest ratings in more than ten years. "We still had some problems," Godwin noted, "but the state could tell from the atmosphere that we were committed to resolving them."

Regrettably, since his departure, the nursing home's ratings have slipped again.

When Godwin left the Houston facility, he became the administrator of a very "high-end" nursing home in Dallas. His former staff in Houston, learning of his new location, took it upon themselves to send a note to the staff of the Dallas facility, telling them how valued they had felt under his leadership and that they had much to look forward to in working with him.

The letter was posted in the new facility and immediately became defaced with comments such as "Who cares?" Once again Godwin had walked into a staff who felt unappreciated and hostile. While there was a core group of devoted staff, many others had left under the previous administration. Word had gotten out about the poor administration of the facility, and it had become difficult to attract high-quality staff. The facility's operations had suffered accordingly.

Godwin immediately told the current staff the following: "If you want to work hard and do a good job, I'll be the best boss you ever had. If you are not interested in taking care of the residents and doing a good job, you probably won't want to stay here."

This pronouncement created quite a stir among the staff, but they would soon learn what he meant. Godwin started demonstrating his commitment by becoming very visible in the facility. For example, before admitting a person who had special needs and might require a high level of special care, Godwin would talk to the staff and ask them, "Do you think you'll be able to take care of this person?" For a nurse's aide to have the executive director ask his or her opinion about admitting a patient was unheard of. The staff immediately felt validated and believed that their opinions and ideas mattered.

In addition to other programs to thank the staff, he instituted Spirit Awards, a way of publicly acknowledging staff for upholding the spirit of the facility in the way they cared for residents. When a resident's family member would stop by Godwin's office to comment on the excellent care provided by a nursing assistant, Godwin admitted, it was tempting to "feel good about the job I'm doing" and let it end there. Instead, he implemented the Spirit Awards: in staff meetings, he would let the staff members who had been complimented by residents' families know how others felt about the care they were giving. He would follow this up by telling them, "And it makes me feel really good to hear those kinds of things from families and to know I'm involved with a facility that offers this kind of service. I really appreciate what you're doing." This was the first time many of the staff had ever been publicly acknowledged for their efforts.

Loyalty among the staff hit an all-time high during Godwin's tenure. And this was in spite of the fact that the facility's budget allowed for only average salaries, while many of his competitors paid a great deal more. "People stayed here for more than a paycheck," Godwin said. "They felt valued for their contributions, and this meant more to them than moving to another facility, where they might make a little more money but would not be appreciated for their service."

Not only must a nursing home do a good job, but the staff must be very customer service–oriented as well. Even in the best facilities, mistakes are made, and if the residents' families are experiencing good customer service and believe the staff are doing the best they can, they tend to be more understanding. Godwin summarized this by citing an old health care saying: "A bad doctor with good bedside manners rarely gets sued, yet good doctors with bad bedside manners get sued all the time." He went on to say, "Of course our goal is to be the good doctor who also has good bedside manners."

The staff's friendliness is important, especially when dealing with the most difficult customers. Godwin told the story of one resident's very difficult family, who gave him the "worst chewing out" of his professional life because his staff did not consistently separate the resident's laundry correctly (specifically, the cottons from the silks). The family found fault with the smallest details in his facility and finally, in frustration, decided to move their mother to another well-respected facility. Within a week and half, the family was back, tearfully asking Godwin to let their mother move back in. Their reason for returning? "All of the staff at your facility are friendly. Everyone goes out of their way to talk to Mother and check up on her. We feel like our mother is loved here." The staff at the other facility might have been more efficient at following rigid instructions, but they weren't friendly, and the personal care and attention were missing. Godwin hastened to add that when the resident moved back in, his staff tried harder to separate the laundry correctly, although this was no longer the family's chief concern.

Godwin knows that the kind of attention this mother received does not come from a nurse's aide who is always being chewed out by his or her boss. He remembered his own experience as a nurse's aide, when his boss had either ignored the line staff or had constantly been negative in her dealings with them. It made it hard for Godwin and his coworkers to be cheerful with the residents when their own boss was seldom cheerful with them.

It was not just the line staff who benefited from his leadership. Godwin included department heads in all key decisions, shared financial information with them, and provided information about issues that in other facilities would be withheld. All this made the department heads feel that they were important and their opinions mattered.

Another way he acknowledged his staff was with a book of gift certificates (to movie theaters, restaurants, grocery stores) that stayed in the front office. If a staff member had worked several double shifts in a time of staff shortages, for example, he would give that person a pair of movie tickets as a thank-you. Bought in bulk, the tickets did not cost much, but the goodwill they earned was priceless. When one of his managers had to work part of several weekends in a row, he gave her a gift certificate to a nice restaurant so that she and her husband could go out. This was a thank-you to both of them for the personal time lost. Compared to the costs of turnover and disgruntlement, these kinds of rewards are inexpensive ways of showing staff that they are appreciated.

Godwin said he had learned about this kind of acknowledgment from a previous boss. When the facility where he worked was given a nice award, his boss said, "You and your wife go out for a nice dinner and bring the receipt back to me and I'll reimburse you." Godwin said that the boss could have offered to take him out to dinner, but it would have meant being out late and away from his family an additional evening; or the boss could have offered to take both Godwin and his wife out to dinner, which would have been nicer. "But the nicest gift," said Godwin, "was when he sent me and my wife out for a relaxing dinner, just the two of us, with none of the pressure of being with the boss."

This kind of acknowledgment is motivating not only for an employee but for the employee's spouse, who becomes more understanding of the sometimes long hours and special circumstances required by certain jobs.

Under Godwin's caring leadership, this facility became the care center of choice for those who could afford it. Almost 100 percent of the families who inquired about the center chose to move their loved one in. Thus, you can imagine Godwin's surprise and dismay when a prospective resident's family chose a competing facility. He asked the family why they had chosen the competitor. They replied that although his building was much better, the other facility had pictures of staff on the walls listing their years of service, many with more than twenty years of service. This family chose what they perceived to be a facility with a more stable staff over the beautiful carpets and chandeliers that Godwin's facility offered.

This was an important lesson for him and reminded him of the plaques at his first facility. Although he had done a lot of positive recognition of his current staff, none of it was visible in public areas for families to see. The lesson was that recognizing staff publicly sends the right message not only to staff but to customers as well.

Due to Godwin's success at this facility, he was then given the opportunity to open and operate the owner company's newest flagship center. A few years later, after realizing his long-term goal of opening his own center, he moved on to what he considered to be his ideal position. A lifelong Presbyterian, he got the opportunity to become the CEO and executive director of the Presbyterian Church's only health care and retirement community in the Dallas area, Grace Presbyterian Village.

Grace Presbyterian Village is a wonderful facility providing excellent care. It is dependent on contributions from the Presbyterian Church, along with residents' fees. This means that much of the glamour of more costly facilities is missing. Also, although it is nestled in a lovely, woodsy setting, it is located in a part of Dallas now populated by mostly low- to middle-income residents.

Godwin, whose parents are both Presbyterian ministers, said he had been attracted to Grace Presbyterian Village because it gave him an opportunity to give back to the community. And it goes without saying that the search committee was delighted to have his level of experience in a leadership role here.

Although at this writing he has been at Grace Presbyterian Village just over a year, he has already begun his programs of staff acknowledgment. He has implemented a Wall of Honor, where photos of and plaques for employees who have served the village from five to almost thirty-five years have been placed. Before prospective staff members are interviewed, they are taken by this wall of photos. Already he has heard prospects say, "This must be a good place to work; look how many people have stayed here for so long."

To both prospective staff and the families of prospective residents, Godwin and his staff point out the stability of the staff honored on the wall. The results have been noticeable. Godwin's comment was "Doing what's right for your staff is also just plain good business."

Godwin explained that the plaques cost only about $12 each (the photographs are done free by a member of his father's church). By comparison, if one additional family chooses Grace Presbyterian Village over its competitors, the potential annual revenue from that person will be anywhere from $14,000 to $50,000 a year. When the potential reduction in turnover costs versus the small cost of providing the plaques is considered, it becomes obvious that it is very cost-effective to honor one's staff in such a way.

It probably won't surprise you that Godwin himself personally enjoys taking prospective staff members, potential residents' family members, and possible donors around the facility for their initial tour. He is careful to point out how much he and the village value the staff, who are responsible for the care the facility's residents receive. He also introduces them to the staff they meet in passing, always commenting on how long they've been there and what good care they give the residents.

One of the ways in which Godwin reminds himself of the importance of daily acknowledgment is by placing ten paper clips in his left-hand pants pocket each morning. Each time he praises a staff member, he moves a paper clip to the right-hand pocket. His goal is to make sure all ten paper clips get moved to the right-hand pocket each day.

On a personal note, when Godwin first arrived at Grace Presbyterian Village, he promised the staff and residents that he would know each of their names within three months. He beat his goal by more than a month. At a recent board of directors meeting, my husband told me, Godwin led a tour of the facility for new board members. True to his word, he called every staff member by name during the tour.

Godwin also reinstated the Perfect Attendance Program, which had been discontinued by his predecessor. Under this program, staff who have perfect attendance for six months were given $100. If they go a year with perfect attendance, they receive an additional $150. He believes this is a small price to pay compared to the overtime paid when staff who don't show up for work must be filled in for.

Godwin went on to say, "Studies have shown that perfect attendance programs tend to reward people who were going to show up anyway. However, if such a program is in place and is then taken away, as it was at the village, it can have a tremendous impact on attendance."

It had also been customary to have an employee picnic. The year Godwin arrived, the picnic had been canceled. When he asked the assistant administrator why the picnic had been canceled, his reply was "It rained that day." When Godwin asked if the picnic had been rescheduled, he was told that it had not. The reason given? "It wasn't our fault it rained." He told the assistant administrator that it *was*, however, his fault that the picnic had not been rescheduled. When the assistant administator responded that they couldn't afford to reschedule the picnic, Godwin responded, "We can't afford not to." That assistant administrator is no longer there.

Godwin clearly sees the correlation between celebrating the accomplishments of one's employees and the bottom line. For example, when a resident compliments a nurse's aide because he or she is doing a good job, that resident is also apt to tell his or her family about the aide's good care. The family, in turn, may mention to someone else what good care their family member is receiving at Grace Presbyterian Village. If that kind of message turns into just one inquiry that turns into an admission, that's another $40,000 a year in revenue.

It's paying attention to the little things that makes Godwin such an affirming administrator. When he decides to do midnight rounds, he always shows up with a box of doughnuts for the staff. Even if there are problems that need to be discussed with staff members, what they remember is that "he didn't come in looking for trouble; he came in positive, expecting the best from us." This approach makes the sometimes necessary counseling much more effective, since the employees know he isn't out to get them.

Godwin developed this positive approach early on and has seen firsthand how much more effective it is than a negative approach. He recounted the story of another administrator who came down very hard on her staff and had a very negative approach to handling personnel problems. Although both

Godwin and his fellow administrator faced the same difficult staff situations, often resulting in the discipline or termination of employees, the results were very different. The other administrator's approach left her employees angry at her, and they showed it by personally threatening her and vandalizing her car on five occasions.

When Godwin finds himself in the position of needing to fire someone, the conversation goes something like this: "I'm sorry we've come to this point. I was excited when you were hired because you demonstrated great potential. I am upset by what has happened because you are a good person." And so on. This approach causes the employee to focus on himself and what he can do differently next time. As a result, Godwin has never been threatened by an angry ex-employee (nor has his car ever been vandalized).

One former employee terminated by Godwin went on to recommend to his friends that they seek employment at Godwin's facility! This person went to work at another facility and told the staff there that if they should ever change jobs, they should go to work for Godwin because he took such good care of his people.

"It's just irresponsible not to take care of staff," Godwin reflects. "For one thing, it makes good business sense. It's also the right thing to do."

Just in the short time he has been at Grace Presbyterian Village, there have been noticeable changes.

I have a vested interest in the success of this facility since it is now home to my mother as well as my in-laws. When I called my mother and asked her to poll her friends on what life has been like at the village since Godwin's arrival, here's what she told me: "Mostly what you notice is a change in the atmosphere. Frowns have been replaced with smiles, and the residents are relaxed instead of tense. We see Godwin everywhere, in the dining room, in the health units, in the hallways, and on the grounds. He's constantly asking residents and staff alike what they need, what they want.

"When he came here, he said it was his intention to know the name of every staff person and every resident within three months. I think he beat his estimate. He calls everyone by name, and that makes us feel good.

"We also like the fact that he's attracted good staff. Everyone is friendly and goes out of their way to help.

"And as far as the facilities themselves, we've heard that Godwin has recruited volunteers and donors from some of the Presbyterian churches in Dallas to help paint and spruce up the cottages for the retirement residents, at no cost to the village."

The environment my mother describes is in sharp contrast to Godwin's own tour of Grace Presbyterian Village two weeks before he was to begin his job as executive director. He toured the facility on his own, which meant that the staff did not know who he was. He recalls that not a single staff person smiled or greeted him. A few glared before looking away, but not a single smile or cheerful greeting was to be found anywhere.

One of the first things he did after he started was to tell the staff that he expected smiles and cheerful greetings. And he models these behaviors himself. He is constantly smiling and greeting people—by name—and they, in turn, follow his lead. They do so not because he demands it, but because he models it by creating an atmosphere in which people feel validated.

My interview with Godwin Dixon ended with his saying, "There are two things that are important above all else when it comes to acknowledging staff. One is that the feedback you give them must be specific. Don't just tell people they're doing a good job; tell them specifically what it is about how they perform their job that is praiseworthy. Second, never underestimate what good recruiters your staff are when they feel appreciated. Word of mouth is the best way to attract and retain the best people."

About this last point, I can personally testify that more than one sad nursing home administrator has lost highly competent staff when they learned that Godwin Dixon had become the administrator at Grace Presbyterian Village and was looking for a few good people.

Thank you, Godwin Dixon, for making Grace Presbyterian Village the kind of place the best people want to work at—and for providing such a loving home for our parents.

CHAPTER FIFTEEN

NOW WHAT?

THE REAL RISK IS TO DO NOTHING.
—DENIS WAITLEY, AUTHOR AND BUSINESS CONSULTANT

Life is full of wonderful opportunities. There are virtually no limits to what we are capable of achieving. Our resources are nearly endless. If we want to lose weight, the bookstores are packed with hundreds of books promising to help us achieve this goal. If we want to start an exercise program, there are books, health clubs, and personal trainers waiting to show us the way. If our goal is to be better organized, seminars, books, and experts are available. In other words, if resources are what we need to help us along the way, there is no shortage. These resources, however, are little more than useless if we don't use them. Buying a book on dieting doesn't help us lose weight if we stop with just reading the book. Likewise, buying a membership at a local gym does little good if we never go there to work out. Attending a seminar on how to be better organized, no matter how brilliant the content, remains only interesting information if we don't put it to use.

The same scenario applies to businesses and organizations whose goal and desire is to create a more affirming workplace. This book is filled with examples and profiles of companies that exceed the expectations of stakeholders (customers, vendors, shareholders, employees) when they put employees' needs first. My friend and former boss, Dr. Stephen R. Covey, wrote a phenomenal best-seller called *The Seven Habits of Highly Effective People* in which he demonstrated time and again what happens at work when effectiveness (with people) takes precedence over efficiency (with things).

Likewise, no organization has the right to plead ignorance when it comes to accomplishing the goal of creating an affirming culture.

This book was written to be a resource for addressing our greatest need next to physical survival, that of knowing we matter as human beings. Our desire to be validated is one of the strongest needs we have. I have also shown that there are substantial payoffs for exercising our acknowledgment muscles, both as individuals and as organizations. This book is intended to be a resource for building upon your desire to acknowledge and be acknowledged, to be affirmed for who and what you are.

As with any resource, however, its usefulness is limited unless you take action on its principles.

If you are like me, when you get excited about introducing something into your life that you know will be beneficial and satisfying, the excitement eventually bumps up against your well-honed habits of procrastination and bowing to competing interests. We're always picking and choosing between that which is good and that which is better, that which is better and that which is best. The very day I vow to start showing up at the gym is also the same day one of my daughters asks me to baby-sit for my grandchildren. I quickly remind myself that there is a lot about being a grandmother in my personal mission statement, so the trip to the gym gets delayed—again. The day I set for eliminating sugar from my diet is the same day I have been asked to direct the bake sale for a church function . . . and I just couldn't ask people to consume all those goodies if I wasn't willing to do so myself. Besides, I can start the cut-out-sugar thing next week. And so what if I spend another month dealing with office clutter—when will I have another chance to take the trip I've planned with a friend? The fact that the "getting organized" seminar is on the same day we're scheduled to depart just means that I'll have to attend the next one. And how about an organization that says it's committed to creating a workplace that honors the contributions of its employees "just as soon as" . . . profits increase, the company's stock value improves, turnover decreases, productivity soars, or there's money in the budget for such a program?

Sound familiar?

All these concerns, whether relating to diet, exercise, organization, or workplace acknowledgment, are valid. But they are not mutually exclusive. In other words, we don't have to choose between profits and praise or between going to the gym and taking care of adored grandchildren. In fact, one can be the impetus for the other, not the barrier that stands in the way. For example, one of the reasons I started a vigorous workout regimen at the gym is so that I would have the energy I need to be an active part of my grandchildren's lives. As many of the companies profiled in this book attest, it is when we honor and celebrate *first* those who work for us that *profits improve, productivity increases,* and *turnover declines.*

This kind of reasoning is what my friend and former business colleague Sharon Fox Hasley calls a "BFO," a blinding flash of the obvious. There is nothing to master here other than the discipline that transforms desire into action. As Mark Twain said, "Even if you're on the right track, you'll get run over if you just sit there."

What, then, does the process of getting started look like? Here are some suggestions to make the discipline of transition easier.

1. Tell the truth about what an absence of acknowledgment costs.

First of all, especially at the organizational level, examine what it's costing you *not* to have an affirming culture. In the workshops I conduct, participants have no problem calculating the bottom-line consequences when acknowledgment is missing. For example, when morale slips because employees don't feel appreciated for their contributions, absenteeism and turnover increase. Most companies can readily assign a dollar value to what those things cost. When creativity is stifled because workers feel their ideas and suggestions are not valued, they often take those ideas to competitors who value what they offer.

Again, the cost to a company when this happens can be quickly calculated. For example, many organizations conduct exit interviews when employees leave voluntarily. For the most part, these interviews are casually done, and little if anything is done with the information they provide. During exit interviews, if employees say that they are leaving for more money, they should be probed to find out if what they are really saying is that they hope that by being paid more they will feel more valued. If this is the case, what they are saying is that the real reason they are leaving is that they don't feel valued, not that they want more money.

Southwest Airlines pays less than its competitors in many job categories. Yet when job openings, including those for pilots, are announced, people line up to apply for the positions, even when the pay is less than what they are currently making!

2. Create a spending plan for the surplus that acknowledgment creates.

While it is important to understand what an absence of acknowledgment is costing you, it is just as important to identify the payoffs when a sustained culture of employee appreciation is in place. As the companies profiled in the book demonstrate, both the hard and soft rewards of acknowledgment can have huge benefits for an organization. Remember First Tennessee Bank and the millions of dollars generated when customer retention increased by 7 percent in the business units run by the managers who did the best job of taking care of their employees? Or the more than $1 million the bank saved in turnover costs over a three-year period? Think of what you could do with all the money saved when turnover and absenteeism are reduced, or with the resources that become available when creativity is unleashed and productivity soars; or what happens to trust when communication is open and honest, rather than withheld. Be very clear about what this means to your organization. Get it down in black and white.

For most companies, deciding what to do with money saved isn't a problem.

3. Cultivate the habit of acknowledgment.

If your goal is to create long-term, sustainable results such as those enjoyed by the organizations profiled in this book, you may need to develop the habit of acknowledgment. Many experts agree that it usually takes thirty days of practice for something to become a habit, whether it's an exercise program or becoming an affirming individual. This is precisely the reason I developed the 30-Day Process. Acknowledging or praising someone at random feels good in the moment, but, unlike sustained acknowledgment, it does little to produce long-term results.

Thirty days can be a stretch, I know. This is the reason Chapter 9 offers a wide variety of ways of celebrating and affirming the value of those around you, to give you an opportunity to develop your acknowledgment muscles over time. Be very clear, however, that the kind of payoffs we're talking about in this book are the results of sustained, intentional efforts. Throwing in the towel or backing out when the going gets tough gets you what you already have and nothing more. Use the guidelines offered in Chapter 4 to get started.

You may want to begin with a specific division or department in your organization and have it complete the 30-Day Process. I invite you to track the results against other departments where there is no acknowledgment initiative.

While it is always preferable to have such an effort begin at the top of an organization, there is no reason to wait to get started. If you are a manager or first-line supervisor, a division director or department head, begin with your area of responsibility. I remember reading an interview with the CEO of a prominent organization shortly after it had received a national quality award. The interviewer asked the CEO if the quality initiative had begun with him. He replied no and explained that there was a rather remote division of the company that had produced extraordinary results because of its quality efforts. He went on to explain that the company had been so impressed with what the division had accomplished that its methods had been implemented companywide. As a result, the company successfully competed for the national quality award.

One word of caution here: You will recall in the chapter explaining the 30-Day Process that there must be no *so that* reasons for initiating the process. The same is true at the organizational level. In other words, a culture of acknowledgment should not be instilled *so that* profits and productivity will increase or turnover and absenteeism will decrease. Rather, those effects will be the natural outcomes of an affirming culture. One should create a workplace culture that appreciates and validates its employees because it is the right thing to do.

4. Share the results!

Remember Tony Harris, the director of diversity and employee relations for BNA, in Chapter 3? His advice for when a company wins an award for being a great place to work is to publicize it! Employees and other stakeholders should be told of the results achieved when acknowledgment is made a workplace priority. It is a great recruitment tool. Spread the word! TDIndustries, for example, hosted a conference last year for other winners of *Fortune* magazine's "100 Best Companies to Work For." The conference provided an opportunity to share best practices, to learn what works and doesn't work in other organizations when it comes to creating an affirming workplace.

Finally, please share your results with me. I'd like to hear about what you are doing or are willing to do to create a culture where who and what people are are richly acknowledged. I would like to know what happens with those of you who try some version of the 30-Day Process, individuals as well as organizations. Please tell me what you learned about yourself as well as others when you tried the process. Let me know about the domino effect, the mirroring effect, and any other results you noticed.

At the back of this book, there is information on how you can contact me with your results. Please give me the opportunity and pleasure of acknowledging you for your commitment and courage.

It is my hope that this book will open the door to a culture and way of being that honors revealing and celebrating the qualities and contributions that others bring to our lives.

I invite you (yes, *you*) to be the person who takes the initiative to start a workplace effort that results in the people in your division, department, or work group mastering the habit of acknowledgment. I invite you to start the 30-Day Process with your spouse, son or daughter, friend, parent, or

other person. You've probably often told yourself that some-
day you'll be on the leading edge of something. Why not
have it be letting those around you know how much you
value their talents and qualities? After all, someone has
noted that we rarely remember the names of last year's
Academy Award winners, but we rarely forget people who
see our goodness and share it with us.

A SUMMARY OF THE 30-DAY PROCESS GUIDELINES

The following is a summary of the 30-Day Process Guidelines found in Chapter 4. It is offered here as a quick reference guide. For more detailed information, you may want to refer to Chapter 4 again.

INSTRUCTIONS

Identify a key relationship at work (or at home). This may be a boss, subordinate, or peer (or friend or family member). Once a day for thirty consecutive days (weekends optional), share with that person a different quality, competence, or trait that you admire, value, and/or appreciate about him or her and offer an example of when you have seen that quality displayed.

Note: It is essential that you complete the number of traits promised. The process—and the relationship—will be jeopardized if you deliver less than promised. Those of you who have a hard time committing to anything for thirty consecutive days may want to commit yourself initially for ten days of traits, then keep increasing that number until you have reached thirty. The full impact of the 30-Day Process doesn't kick in until about two weeks after you've started, so staying with it for thirty traits is imperative.

GUIDELINES

1. Select someone whom you see daily or can contact on a regular enough basis to accomplish the process over a thirty-day period. While the traits can be shared by phone or e-mail, the impact is *much greater* when they are shared in person. The first time you try this process, it is wise to select a relationship that is healthy and stable, one that is good and that you want to make better.

2. Set a context for sharing the process with your partner. *Tell that person what you are doing.* Tell him or her that you are committed to doing a better job of letting the people around you know how much they are valued, and you have selected him or her as part of this commitment. Let that person know that once a day for the next thirty (or ten) days, you would like to share a different trait or quality that you admire and appreciate about him or her.

3. Set an agreed-upon time and place for the daily sharing. Failure to do so often results in confusion.

4. Ask your partner to accept what you share without demurring or becoming defensive. It is human nature for people to say things like "That's not how I see myself" or "You must be kidding!" Remind your partner that you are sharing your perspective of him or her. If he or she must say something, "Thanks" is sufficient.

5. It is not necessary—or even recommended—that all the traits be identified before you start the process. In fact, discovering some of the traits along the way is one of the most insightful aspects of the process. In most instances, traits you hadn't noticed before will surface and you can add them to the list as you go along. *Note:* Some of you will "run out" of traits before the thirty days is up. This is not due to a shortage of qualities on the part of your partner; rather, it is a signal that your own powers of observation need to be sharpened. Trust me when I say that there are *always* at least thirty things to admire in each of us.

6. It is a good idea to keep a list of the traits as you go along. By the end of the process, it is easy to forget which traits have already been shared and which have not.

7. If you find that you have skipped a day of sharing for whatever reason, it is better not to double up the next time but rather to extend the agreed-upon time period an extra day or so. Doing otherwise dilutes the full impact of the sharing.

8. Since you will be doing the 30-Day Process with someone you know relatively well, Murphy's Law pretty much guarantees that "stuff" will come up that will annoy you about the other person or otherwise get in the way of your sharing. If this happens, remember that your partner's qualities exist *independently of your feelings about that person* at any particular time. Be consistent with who they are rather than with your own feelings when they conflict.

9. Participate in the process for the joy and rewards of acknowledging another, not *so that* the other person will change, like you better, promote you, and so on.

10. Expect the relationship to be transformed, especially in the nature and authenticity of future communication.

11. Once you have shared thirty qualities, bring closure to the process by thanking your partner for participating—and you might just want to pat yourself on the back for completing this important adventure!

If you are interested in providing feedback once you have completed the process, please log on to www.dottiegandy.com, where you will find an electronic feedback form for both you and your partner. Your insights and suggestions are an important part of my ongoing research into the value of acknowledgment.

FREQUENTLY CITED TRAITS

The following is a list of the traits most frequently cited by respondents who have completed the 30-Day Process and provided me with feedback. It is offered for those of you who may have trouble putting a name to a behavior or quality. You may list traits that do not appear here, which is to be expected and quite acceptable. This list should be used to prod your thinking.

Accepting	Athletic
Accommodating	Attracts love
Accountable	Authentic
Adventuresome	Available
Affable	Awesome
Always growing	Baker
Ambitious	Balanced
Analytical	Beautiful
Anchor	Best friend
Animal lover	Bilingual
Appreciative	Bright
Articulate	Budget manager
Artist	Business owner
Assertive	Calming presence

Calm spirit

Caring

Caring stepparent

Celebrates special occasions

Champion

Charitable

Cheerful

Chef

Childlike

Church servant

Classy

Clean

Clever

Coach

Colorful

Comfortable

Committed

Community servant

Compassionate

Compatible

Complimentary

Computer whiz

Confident

Conscientious

Considerate

Consistent

Contagious laughter

Contemplative

Cool

Cooperative

Copilot

Courageous

Courteous

Creative

Curious

Decorator

Dedicated

Deep

Dependable

Desirable

Detached

Determined

Devoted

Difference maker

Direct

Disciplined

Distinguished

Efficient

Emotionally strong

Empathic

Encouraging

Enduring

Enjoys life

Enjoys life, beauty, and so on

Enterprising

Entertaining

Enthusiastic

Ethical

Even-tempered

Expressive

Exuberant

Fair

Faithful

Family-oriented

Fearless

Fights for kids

Flexible

Forgiving

Friendly

Fulfills dreams

Full of laughter

Fun

Generous

Generous spirit

Gentle

Gets the job done

Gifted

Giving

Good cook

Good neighbor

Graceful

Gracious

Great friend/dad/mom

Gung ho

Handsome

Handyman

Hard worker

Healer

Health-conscious

Healthy

Helpful

High-energy

Honest

Honorable

Household steward

Humble

Humorous

Idea generator

Inclusive

Inquisitive

Insightful

Intellectual

Intelligent

Intense

Internal drive

Introspective

Intuitive

Joyful

Just

Kind

Knowledgeable

Leader

Lovable

Lovely

Loving

Loyal

Mediator

Mentor

Merciful

Messenger of God

Metaphysical

Moderate

Modest

Money manager

Moral

Musician

Music lover

Neat

Nonjudgmental

Nurturing

Obedient

Observant

Open-minded

Orderly

Organized

Pal

Partner

Passionate

Patient

Patriotic

Peaceful

Persevering

Persistent

Person of faith

Physically fit

Pleasant

Positive

Principle-centered

Problem solver

Professional

Proud

Public presenter/speaker

Punctual

Purposeful

Quick learner

Quick to forgive

Quick-witted

Receives feedback well

Receptive

Reflective

Reliable

Resilient

Resourceful

Respected

Respectful

Responsible

Responsive

Rethinks and apologizes

Reverent

Risk taker

Rolls with the punches

Romantic

Runner

Safe harbor

Seeker

Self-aware

Self-disciplined

Self-reliant

Self-starter

Sense of humor

Sensitive

Service-oriented

Singer

Skillful

Smart

Solution-oriented

Special

Spiritual

Spiritual leader

Spontaneous

Steadfast

Steady

Strong

Student

Stylish

Supportive

Sweet

Tactful

Teacher

Team player

Technologically competent

Tenacious

Tender

Thankful

Thorough

Tolerant

Trusting

Trustworthy

Truthful

Unconditionally loving

United

Unselfish

Values family

Vegetarian

Versatile

Visionary

Vulnerable

Walks his or her talk

Warmhearted

Well groomed

Well-ordered priorities

Whimsical

Wise

Word keeper

Worthy

Writer

Young at heart

Youthful

Zealous

A SAMPLE LIST OF THIRTY TRAITS

The following is a sample of what thirty traits might look like, along with a possible example of each. This list is a model only. The traits have been alphabetized, although it is unlikely that your own sharing will be in any sort of order, alphabetical or otherwise. I offer this list simply as an example to help some of you get started.

1. *Accepting:* Meets people where they are; tolerates many views.

2. *Accountable:* Holds himself or herself responsible for results.

3. *Ambitious:* Volunteers regularly for additional assignments.

4. *Appreciative:* Expresses gratitude to others for a job well done.

5. *Articulate:* Expresses himself or herself clearly, especially on difficult subjects.

6. *Balanced:* Models what it means to value work and personal life equally.

7. *Calm:* Remains unflustered in difficult situations.

8. *Cheerful:* Has a friendly spirit; is always in a good mood; is fun to be around.

9. *Coach/mentor:* Supports the effectiveness of others by helping them find solutions to their problems.

10. *Community servant:* Volunteers in the community.

11. *Compassionate:* Is sympathetic to the concerns and issues of others.

12. *Conscientious:* Is not one to cut corners; makes sure all bases are covered.

13. *Dependable:* Can be counted on to keep his or her commitments.

14. *Enthusiastic:* Knows how to keep a team's energy up.

15. *Even-tempered:* Keeps his or her cool; isn't driven by extreme emotions.

16. *Flexible:* Knows how to roll with the punches; can be counted on to go with the team's decisions.

17. *Generous:* Is always willing to share knowledge and time with others.

18. *Honest:* Is up front; does not engage in two-faced conversations.

19. *Humorous:* Uses humor appropriately, especially to ease tension.

20. *Insightful:* Knows how to find the "nugget" of a problem that will solve it.

21. *Leader:* Sees the big picture and shares it with the team.

22. *Mission-driven:* Honors the mission of the organization and makes decisions accordingly.

23. *Problem solver:* Sees it as his or her responsibility to provide solutions.

24. *Professional:* Represents the team and the company well in a wide variety of situations.

25. *Punctual:* Can be counted on to show up on time; honors time commitments.

26. *Resourceful:* Always seems to know where to look when additional ideas or tools are needed.

27. *Sensitive:* Is conscious of the feelings of others and behaves accordingly.

28. *Student:* Is always in a learning mode; looks for ways to strengthen his or her competencies and knowledge.

29. *Thorough:* His or her reports are always well researched.

30. *Trustworthy:* Can be counted on to put first things first.

Dear Reader,

If you are interested in providing feedback on how you and/or your organization did with the 30-Day Process described in this book, if you are interested in learning more about the seminar based on this book, or if you want to contact me regarding a speaking engagement, here's how to do so:

Dottie Gandy
www.dottiegandy.com

Your interest in making this a more affirming world in which to live is greatly appreciated.

Sincerely,

Dottie Gandy